# The
# Motivated Brain

**Helle Bundgaard**

**Jefferson Roy**

# THE MOTIVATED BRAIN

ISBN-13: 978-1499698374

ISBN-10: 1499698372


Published in collaboration with:

Motivation Factor ApS
Symbion Science Park
Fruebjergvej 3
DK-2100 København Ø
Denmark

# Thanks

First and foremost I want to express my heartfelt gratitude to Julie Lynch, my business partner and friend. She has been by my side since I did my first Motivation Factor training in the US in 2009. Never failing to believe that this would make an impact in the world, she has been an invaluable resource in helping me write this book.

I also want to thank my coauthor Jefferson Roy. I met Jefferson on a Motivation Factor certification I did in Copenhagen back in 2011. When I asked him to help us write a whitepaper linking Motivation Factor to neuroscience he replied, "What do you need me for; it works".

Well, long story short, that became the beginning of a long series of conversations and professional discussions, and finally we agreed that he should be my coauthor in supporting the scientific link to the Motivation Factor Framework.

My deep appreciation goes to all the others, who have made this book possible.

# Feedback

If you have any good ideas or suggestion for new books in this context, or any feedback at all, I would love to hear from you.

Please send me an email to hb@motivationfactor.com

## Free Motivation Assessment

We encourage you to do the Motivation Factor Indicator, our online assessment that puts words to your 10 most important motivation factors in form of your Top 5 needs and Top 5 talents.

You get free access to the motivation assessment Motivation Factor Indicator by sending an email to brain@motivationfactor.com and in the subject line write "Free Indicator 90614".

# The Motivated Brain

# Chapter 1: Introduction

We are all eager to crack the code for sustained motivation, but despite the great pool of motivation books available, few succeed in the long term. This owes mainly to the fact that most approaches to motivation focus on self-motivation and one-size-fits all prescriptions, which at best address only part of the equation. Modern psychological theories acknowledge the deeply personal aspects of motivation, yet the practical advice of most business books does not factor those into their recommended solutions.

Of particular interest at the moment are books focused on strengths-based approaches, the question of meaningful Purpose, and what neuroscientists currently can tell us about the function of our brains. I have read a lot of very good books, each addressing their own area within the field of emotional intelligence, positive psychology, theory of flow, and management in general. I couldn't agree more that these are important components in working with and understanding motivation. What I have been missing, though, is a book that pulls all of this together and provides an easy framework and some applicable tools that make it easy to implement in everyday life.

My ambition was to write a book that was easy to read and shared the tools that my partners and I have used so successfully since 2007. But I also wanted to give the reader a profound understanding about WHY this works. To do this I enlisted the help of Jefferson Roy, a neuroscientist, to have him write the link between The Motivation Factor Framework and neuroscience.

## How to read this book

Chapters 1 - 5 cover the introduction, ideas and underlying concept behind the Motivation Factor tools.

Chapters 6 - 9 cover each level of the Hierarchy of Motivation. In each chapter you will be provided with a toolbox that is easy adaptable in both your private and working environment.

Chapter 10 covers the neuroscience supporting the Hierarchy of Motivation and the toolboxes.

## Get a free Motivation Factor Indicator

Before you read further in this book, I encourage you to do the Motivation Factor Indicator, our online assessment that puts words to your 10 most important motivation factors expressed as your Top 5 needs and Top 5 talents.

You get free access to the assessment by sending an email to brain@motivationfactor.com. In the subject line, please write, "Free Indicator 90614".

You can write your Top 5 needs and Top 5 talents here:

| Needs | Talents |
|---|---|
| | |
| | |
| | |
| | |

# Chapter 2: Getting Ready

"What the hell does it take to keep you here?" my director shouted, slamming his fist on his desk. This was understandable behavior, considering this was the third time I'd resigned from his department in as many years. I was one of those sought-after "industry talents", constantly being wooed away by recruiters from other firms. They always offered some new bright shiny object that would catch my attention. "Would THIS be the job that truly motivates me?" I wondered. I would hop around from job to job without ever being clear as to what was so attractive about the new opportunity. Each new offer just felt "more exciting".

What was missing? It wasn't the basics: I was paid handsomely, had a great working environment and wonderful colleagues. It wasn't interest: I was involved in challenging assignments, was using my talents and was recognized for my efforts regularly. It wasn't trying: In terms of further career growth, I would often sit the night before my annual employee review, wracking my brain for something to write in the space on the review form labeled "development".

Since you are expected to have a certain degree of self-awareness, of course I couldn't leave it blank, so I would fill in the space with the names of more or less qualified courses – hoping for the best. My director was supportive and I'm sure he felt some relief at not having to guess what might contribute to my development. After all, who could expect the manager to come up with something that the employee herself is not able to articulate? We never got to the core of what motivated me.

If I had the knowledge then that I have today, I could have avoided a number of wrong job changes and saved companies millions of dollars. Not only the costs associated with hiring and training a new employee, but also the less tangible costs of having an employee who is unmotivated and does not perform optimally. My director would have been saved many headaches as well. His pounding fist that day nearly sent me into a panic. I was unable to answer him. I knew that if I wanted a higher salary, bigger car, more management responsibility, or greater freedom, he would gladly oblige. What on earth did I want? His question was my own.

Little did he - or I – know that his outburst had sown the seeds for what would become the Hierarchy of Motivation, the Motivation Factor framework and the book you now hold in your hands. It was the beginning of a journey that would result in a practical, reproducible way to mobilize lasting motivation.

Motivation fascinates us, not only because of the power it gives us to move forward, but also because it seems so difficult to tap into in a sustained manner. That tension has produced a great deal of thoughtful study and writing and a lot of motivational speakers, techniques, and tips, but lasting results still seem elusive.

Motivation is the driving force behind any kind of action or lack of action. Everything we do stems from motivation – from getting out of bed to winning the top sales person of the year award. We use the word freely: "I need to get motivated" or "I'm not motivated" or "That just doesn't motivate me." We know it's the impetus for our actions and it is the culprit when we fail to act. But when we ask what motivation is and where it comes from, we can't answer. It is fundamental yet undefined.

A good friend of mine had been working at a company for fifteen years. She loved the company, her job, her co-workers, and she was quite happy and enthusiastically committed to helping the company grow and profit. One night, while traveling on business, she encountered what she calls a Resume Generating Experience. One of the leaders of the company – someone she liked and respected – took her to task. At a social gathering in front of her colleagues, he questioned her work and accused her of being lazy and uncommitted. Stunned, hurt and embarrassed, she kept herself composed until she was able to excuse herself from the party and get to her hotel room, whereupon she burst into tears. The next thing she did was open her computer, get online, type www.monster.com and begin searching for a new job.

Motivation sneaks up on us. It is powerful and can spring from seemingly nowhere. Moments before the incident, my friend would have told you she was highly motivated by her work and her company. Moments after the incident, she was highly motivated to leave. But what compelled my friend to act is not necessarily what would compel you or me. The incident that spurred my friend into a job-hunting frenzy may not even hit the radar screen for someone else. Motivation is individual and situational.

Finally, motivation is precious. We can all recall a time when we felt on top of our game, totally committed and pumped full of positive energy for the task at hand. We've all had the experience of being drawn deeper and deeper into the creative project, challenging assignment or compelling argument that is our job at that moment. Where does time go when we are in this "zone", when all our attention and interest, skill and talent are sharply focused and distractions fade away?

As managers responsible for the productivity and performance of our teams, our ability to motivate others and inspire deep commitment is essential. But where does that motivation come from? How can we capture it, harness it, direct it?

If motivation is universal yet individual and situational, if it has no inherent substance and if we are each affected differently by different things, what is the common denominator? I decided to leave my job and dedicate myself to unlocking this mystery. I spent four years learning about the latest developments in psychology and brain science.

In all my research I always kept a practical perspective in mind: How could I relate this to what I knew from being in the trenches as an executive in a high-tech company? What could be easily implemented in the daily work of a manager or individual contributor? What could be done that didn't require us to learn a whole new terminology, categorize individuals into various types, or double up on entitlement programs?

I sought to create a very simple framework that would draw from what is universally human: The fundamentals of how our brain works, and how we process information both emotionally and intellectually. The framework I have developed works across culture, gender, age and vocation because fundamentally, the way the brain processes information is the same for all of us. Regardless of culture or upbringing, we all have the same hardware – the brain. But, of course, what is unique to each of us is the information and experiences that form our worldview.

We can think of these unique inputs as our software – how we internalize, interpret and respond to our environment. The extent to which we each understand and manage our own emotional responses and rational thought processes is also expressly individual. What I have done is put together a framework that works with the universal hardware of the brain while providing tools to manage the software of our motivational drivers. The framework and tools outlined in this book will help you as a manager and individual become a power user of your own brain. Ultimately, you will help yourself and others stay motivated and committed.

The practices outlined in this book are universally applicable because we human beings have a great deal in common. We all face people and situations that drain our energy; we all have a unique set of deeply rooted psychological needs that drive and shape our behavior; we all have specific and uniquely honed talents to offer; and finally, we share that very human search for purpose in our lives.

The exercises I share here provide a practical and reliable way to address Energy Drainers, more effectively manage Needs, release and leverage Talents and – critically – provide that much needed connection to Purpose. This book gives you a simple way to connect employees with a shared goal and identify what their contribution will be toward achieving it. In the face of shifting goals, the managers and leaders who are able to tune into and turn up for what motivates people from within will be the winners.

This is where my thinking on motivation departs from much that has been written on the subject for a business audience. There has been an overemphasis on external fixes and blanket prescriptions that don't recognize individual differences and fail to address the source of people's behavior. Conventional approaches to motivation focus on controlling external factors – money, fear, a sense of security – and often offer one-size-fits-all solutions that don't quite fit anyone.

The tools you will learn in this book are anchored in the "Hierarchy of Motivation" – a model I developed to train individuals to manage their own motivation. You might find that some of it is familiar because I've drawn on the work of well-known psychologists and neuroscientists. What I've sought to do with the Hierarchy of Motivation is to distill these rich concepts into a framework that is simple and easy to work with, but which maintains the transformative power of those complex ideas.

# Chapter 3: Can We Mass Motivate

When we look at how organizations have typically tried to crack the code of motivation, we see attempts at mass motivation. Employee benefits, sales incentives, corporate communications and team building are crafted to appeal to the majority, despite evidence that not everyone is motivated by onsite daycare, a trip to Hawaii, or a personal message from the CEO.

Companies invest millions of dollars bringing in sports stars, celebrities or famed motivational speakers to tell their stories of dizzying accomplishment and how they maintain peak motivation to reach their goals. While it can be very inspiring to listen to a sports legend or celebrity, how many of us can identify with their way of life? Are they also fetching their children from daycare after a workday filled with conflicts and difficult colleagues? Are they shopping, cooking and mowing the lawn before they step out to train for the world championship?

At worst, these attempts to foster motivation can have the opposite effect. To make us listen to someone who oozes self-confidence and surplus energy, while we feel totally overwhelmed and drained, is like waiving a red scarf in front of a bull. I don't know about you, but I have read lots of motivational books and participated in many pep talks and seminars on this subject without really grasping the concept, simply because it was too complex, too exhausting, too much work, or didn't really connect with my beliefs. So what is wrong with me, I might ask. Why does it work for them and not for me? I felt as though I was given the recipe, only to find out that I didn't have the ingredients or the time to cook the meal.

Motivation is deeply personal and resonant. It is not something that can be applied like a spray tan. So the answer to the question "Can you mass motivate people?" is no. We knew this, of course. In so many other facets of business and life, we have seen evidence that in order to compel someone to make a decision or change a behavior, we have to make it personal.

When a group attempts to build its membership, they don't head to the town square, make a speech and expect everyone to sign on. Organizations who successfully recruit and retain members use a carefully crafted strategy to identify target audiences, screen in ideal member profiles and appeal personally to those deemed most receptive to their message.

Political campaigns develop a custom message for each community to appeal across geographies, age groups, affiliations and class. Research shows that voters look for candidates who "understand" their circumstances and "connect" with them on key issues. The saying "All politics is local" speaks to the necessity of understanding and appealing to people's individual concerns.

Decades of product marketing research show that the more targeted the message, the greater the likelihood that customers will buy. Soundly run companies don't pump money into marketing a new product without knowing their market. Indeed, it is well established that the more you know your target group and appeal personally to them, the more success you have. And yet many companies will spend a great deal of money on inspirational pep-talks, incentives and other motivational initiatives that deliver only short term effects – if they work at all.

With all the information we have about motivation and management, why do we still struggle so much with this issue? It's quite clear, actually. In our efforts to simplify we have searched for the universal "code" for motivation. Though it is common sense that individual motivation can't be handled in a generic way, we don't have time for anything but! We don't have time to delve into each and every individual's unique motivators and so, in the absence of that, we'll accept the latest theory on general motivation as the next best thing.

Personality tests, typologies and behavioral assessments abound in the business world. Approaches exist that categorize leaders one way, sales people another, administrative assistants yet another. Other models give us tips on how to interact with different "types". While we may gain insight into others and ourselves by using such tests and perhaps even find some practical techniques for improving our productivity and interpersonal relationships, these systems are flawed.

They all work by tagging and labeling people with a predetermined set of traits, orientations, inclinations or behaviors and at worst, people will disavow responsibility for their behaviors or attitude, using the system as an excuse: "Well, I'm an LMNO type, so what do you expect?" Motivation is not limited by functional norms, personality type or behavioral inclination. It is a dynamic process that is personal and situational, and on which we have much more influence than we realize.

This is why so many motivation and commitment initiatives have failed to make much of a lasting impact. Even though motivation and management theory has acknowledged the individual aspect of motivation and even gone so far as to provide ways to type and catalog different sets of motivators, behaviors and styles, we still end up with what amounts to a one-size-fits-all approach.

The mass motivation approach may give us short-term results. Our incentive programs and attractive benefits may earn us a place on the "Best Places to Work" lists. But in the long run, it is simply not effective. Motivation is a complex interplay of factors unique to each of us requiring personal connection and dynamic management. This sounds complex. It doesn't have to be.

The next few chapters will provide deeper insight into what our motivation factors are, how they work, and where you have much greater leverage than you may have realized in terms of identifying and managing motivation. So follow me to the next chapter in which I give you a framework you can use to recognize what is getting in the way of motivation and what is available to fuel it. Knowledge in itself is worth nothing if you are not able to put it into practice.

# Chapter 4: The M Factor - Mobilizing Lasting Motivation

Much of our current-day thinking on motivation management is still rooted in the work on this subject produced in the mid-20th century. From Abraham Maslow's Hierarchy of Needs[1,2] which introduced the concept of human motivation; to Frederick Herzberg, who became one of the most influential names in business management for introducing his Dual Factor Theory[3] for managing both extrinsic and intrinsic motivators; and to Daniel Pink, author of the very popular book "Drive: The Surprising Truth About What Really Motivates Us"[4], who makes an important and convincing case that intrinsic motivators rather than extrinsic remuneration are key to high performance and satisfaction.

Herzberg's research demonstrated that people will strive to achieve 'hygiene' factors because they are unhappy without them, but once satisfied, the effect soon wears off - satisfaction is temporary. He found that people are only truly motivated by enabling them to reach for and satisfy the factors that Herzberg identified as real motivators; job satisfiers such as achievement, advancement, development, etc., which represent a far deeper level of meaning and fulfillment.

Interestingly, not only do Hygiene Factors fail to motivate people, Herzberg's research showed that Hygiene Factors are cyclical in nature and come back to a starting point. This leads to the "What have you done for me lately?" syndrome. In addition, Hygiene Factors have an escalating zero point and no final answer. This does not bode well for our current approach of mass motivation. Sales incentives, vacation days and ice cream parties may only exacerbate the cyclical and escalating nature of hygiene factor satisfaction.

More recently, Pink makes an important and convincing case that intrinsic motivators rather than extrinsic remuneration are key to high performance and satisfaction. Pink has studied the latest brain research and modern motivation theory and posits that what truly motivates us is having a sense of Purpose, Mastery and Autonomy. In his book, he goes on to provide managers with ideas for developing the conditions for intrinsic motivation in the workplace.

The models mentioned above show a strong progression toward acknowledging and addressing the intrinsic Needs of human beings in the workplace. Pink goes further to encourage conversations with individuals to explore what Purpose, mastery and autonomy mean to them personally, and how they might achieve each in their respective jobs.

These theorists agree that human motivation is impacted by primary or more basic factors such as safety, security, salary and a pleasant working environment, and also by secondary or higher motivators such as meaningful work, achievement, independence and recognition. From this body of work, we have seen organizations put into place a host of environmental improvements from minimum wage and competitive benefits to open door policies, team building and participative management practices. In addition to these, companies have also introduced reward and recognition programs, succession and career planning, training and development efforts and employee satisfaction surveys. This is good progress.

Given this earlier research, we might think that by providing the general conditions for both extrinsic and intrinsic motivation we can ensure a motivated workforce. But consider the enlightened company that puts into place a reward and recognition program, for instance. The program, created with input from a volunteer committee of employees, includes encouraging team members to present hand written "thank you" cards to colleagues who have gone above and beyond the call of duty.

Those who receive a certain number of thank you cards are entered into a drawing for a prize, and their names are announced at the monthly company meeting. Of course, this will be right on target for some percentage of the employee population. Another percentage will be downright hostile to it. The problem is that these types of rewards – such as salary, benefits and ice cream parties - are still, by definition, extrinsic motivators. Worse, we are ignoring the individual and situational nature of personal human motivation and, instead, applying these rewards en masse.

Even with decades of motivation management theory, we still have a one-size-fits-all approach. What is meaningful work to you may not be to me. That which I am interested in being able to do differs from that which interests you. That which I am prepared to achieve and interested in achieving may change over time and across contexts. We still do not have a simple, practical way to generate personal appeal – to ensure true connection between the unique, complex and dynamic motivation factors of the individual and his or her job.

We managers may do our best to create a motivating environment based on the research by Herzberg, Pink and others, but the pitfalls are endless. Even with best intentions, the environment we create will reflect our own motivators or the motivators of a select few – not the motivators of all. Or, in our efforts to appeal to the masses, we may overinvest – offering a virtual smorgasbord of potentially motivating benefits and employment conditions when, in fact, that which your star employees need is one particular elixir not found on the table. The mud-against-the-wall-approach doesn't work. Indeed, as Stephen R.

Covey has said: *"Motivation is a fire from within. If someone else tries to light that fire under you, chances are it will burn very briefly."*

Extrinsic motivators are necessary. Intrinsic motivation is crucial. Yet we don't have the luxury of time to weave a custom solution for each person. We need a simple way to engage each unique individual's motivation factors toward the situation at hand. Of course, you may be thinking "Couldn't we simply ask?" This is a very reasonable question and one that I have asked myself. Is it as simple as asking, "What motivates you?" and then acting accordingly? To test that theory, I invite you to try it here and now. Please take the next few minutes and list five things that motivate you.

In your attempt just now, you may have found yourself thinking back to specific times, people or contextual examples of situations when you felt motivated. That seems to be the best we can do in most cases – to describe a situation that was motivating, a manager or mentor who was able to inspire us, a project or task that we found compelling. Very rarely will someone answer with a definitive word or name for the specific internal condition that was the motivating factor. In my own work as a manager, in my own experiences hopping from job to job looking for that elusive passion, in my years of coaching hundreds of executives, I have found that the answer to the question "do we know ourselves what motivates us?" is "no" – at least not precisely, or practically applicable.

So if hygiene factors are not enough, and the mass application of general conditions to support intrinsic motivation is not enough, and we cannot be trusted to know or articulate our own personal motivators, then what are the true ingredients for sustained personal motivation? From the research at hand – including unprecedented information from the fields of brain research and neuropsychology, it seems that there are three components.

As we've learned from motivation theorists, we do need to offer (but it is not enough to provide) extrinsic motivators. In addition, it is imperative to acknowledge and support intrinsic motivators such as meaningful work, achievement and recognition. This does get us farther down the road toward influencing employee motivation. But in order to develop true self-sustaining personal motivation, we need to add one more ingredient. Combining the existing body of work with nearly ten years of study and practice in personal motivation, I have identified the missing link: Motivation Capability.

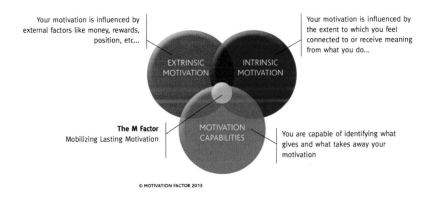

The core of this model for mobilizing lasting motivation is what we call "The M Factor". It is the condition created when extrinsic motivators are satisfied, intrinsic motivation is high and Motivation Capability is present. We each have our own unique M-Factor for mobilizing personal motivation and only the individual can identify what that is to him or her.

The M Factor Model illustrates the simple, iterative, highly individual discipline of making sure one is on the right track and has the resources necessary for success. By applying the model, each individual becomes equipped to analyze and adjust to his or her circumstances as things change. When opportunities or challenges arise in the environment, you now have a "home base" from which to strategize your position and next moves. Let's take a look at each of the components and then see how they work together.

## Extrinsic Motivation

What it is: Those externally supplied conditions that meet our basic or minimum Needs. As Maslow, Herzberg and Pink have all argued, these conditions are necessary to avoid dissatisfaction. Extrinsic motivation is fueled by primary Needs like salary, benefits, and a pleasant working environment. It can also include things like competition or incentive – any externally applied stimulus that prompts us to act.

What it looks like:

- The salesperson "hungry" for financial incentives and therefore highly motivated to close sales.
- The star employee whose family depends on the health benefits offered by the company.

Extrinsic motivation works well in the short term and when the external motivator has personal and near-term value as defined by the recipient. On the other hand, extrinsic motivators can result in unintended behaviors. For example, the sales person might focus on her own need for financial success instead of the customer's need for an efficient solution, leading to low customer satisfaction. Or what happens if your star employee no longer needs to work because his or her spouse gets a job with better health insurance? As Herzberg and others have pointed out, extrinsic motivators are necessary but not enough and, moreover, have an escalating threshold for minimum satisfaction.

## Intrinsic Motivation

What it is: Those internally defined and determined conditions that contribute to the satisfaction of the higher or secondary Needs of achievement, recognition and meaningful work. Intrinsic motivation is based on taking pleasure in an activity itself rather than working towards an external reward. Intrinsic motivation is critical for long-term, sustained motivation – it is deeply personal, situational and can only be identified and articulated by the individual him or herself.

What it looks like:

- The museum art curator whose life-long passion it is to discover, analyze, restore and preserve precious artifacts.
- The employee who loves doing research and adding details.

Intrinsic motivation is inherently energizing and so, going above and beyond, making a difference and contributing to the organization is not a matter of effort but of interest.   On the other hand, intrinsic motivators can put us in conflict with competing realities.  For instance, when the art curator is resistant to and inflexible towards museum patrons who want to view or interact with works of art when the employee cannot meet deadlines because there is always something that needs further investigation.

## Motivation Capability

What it is: The competency of identifying and articulating one's own motivation factors, understanding the influence of those factors on current conditions, and actively managing those factors to result in a more ideal situation. Motivation Capability is vigilance, competence and Purposeful action. It is a meta-awareness of one's own motivation and what can be done to manage it. It is defined as the competency of getting and staying motivated toward one's work regardless of the presence of positive or negative intrinsic and extrinsic factors.

What it looks like:

- The seasoned journalist who has embraced a new way of working as the company transitions from print publications to digital media.

- The star employee who is able to quickly determine that the opportunity presented by the headhunter is not going to offer a more satisfying situation than the one she has with your company.

This third component – Motivation Capability - is what we've been missing in traditional approaches to organizational motivation and engagement. It may be helpful, then, to delve deeper into one of the above scenarios to see Motivation Capability in action.

The print magazine journalist may be well paid, have good benefits and enjoy work as a feature writer. She has the opportunity to interview important people in the industry and communicate critical information to her audience. She enjoys investigating all angles of a story, taking the time to confirm sources and create a compelling argument. Extrinsic and intrinsic motivation is clearly present. Then, from the publisher's office come cries of "Print is dying! We must go digital! We must be first to break news! Fast! Attention-getting! Brief and to the point!" What, you might guess, is the impact on our seasoned journalist? Of course her intrinsic motivation is under threat, her status as a seasoned professional is put into question and she may worry about her ability to remain employed if so much of her skills and training is no longer called for.

Some typical responses in such situations:

- "Bah! This is a phase. I'll ignore it and it'll go away"

- "They don't care about journalistic integrity? I'm out of here!"

- "Well, I'll do it but I'm telling you, it's not going to work"

If, in contrast, our journalist is equipped with Motivation Capability, she can more efficiently analyze her situation and respond in a way that both preserves her own motivation and meets the organizational goals. So equipped, she will actively identify and address the specific aspects of the situation that are detracting from her motivation; she will understand and manage her instinctual response (resistance) to change, she will quickly identify the unique Talents she can call on to get re-engaged in the new reality, and she will analyze and confirm how the new situation might morph into different, but just as meaningful work. Or, she may come to the decision that this new circumstance will not make the best use of her own or the organization's time and Talents and hence, she may choose to seek a new position. In either case, she has served both herself and the organization well.

Another example of Motivation Capability in action is its influence on the impact of life events outside of work. Imagine that an employee has adequate salary and benefits, respectful workplace and supervision. He feels connected to the organization and that the work he does is meaningful. He sees good Purpose in what he does and he contributes his Talents regularly. What happens if the company asks him to relocate or his spouse loses her job? With Motivation Capability, our employee is more quickly able to assess his work and life obligations, identify priorities and put a plan into place.

Going back to my own frustrating story of job-hopping. Each time I was contacted by a headhunter, all the external motivation factors were in place: salary, benefits, extra vacation and more. My Talents were well utilized and recognized regularly, and I was growing and developing, taking on new challenges in my role. But still, I would be motivated to say yes to a position only to find myself in the exact same place six months later. The environment was new, the work assignment was new, the colleagues were new; I was the only thing that wasn't new. My context had changed but I didn't. I didn't become any wiser about why I was so attracted to the new opportunity, or what I felt it was going to give me. I wasn't able to get to the root of the problem. If I had been equipped with Motivation Capability, I would have had a simple way to put words to what motivated me, what was missing, and what I could do about it.

The motivation we get from external and intrinsic motivation factors is never permanent, because our environment is always changing. If something in the environment changes (becoming parents, a call from a headhunter, a reprimand from a company leader, a divorce) something goes missing or is put under pressure. Without the Motivation Capabilities to identify the reason behind what you are experiencing and what you can do about it, you will be more driven by – and compelled to act in response to – temporal, situational and external factors. Conversely, when you have Motivation Capability, you are more easily able to determine what factors are in play, whether the situation has a short term or long term impact, and what you might do about it to return to or attain a more ideal situation.

You might wonder how important this concept of Motivation Capability is to the health and vitality of your business. IDG Research and Motivation Factor Institute conducted a study combining a traditional employee satisfaction survey with the Motivation Factor PinPointer – a questionnaire designed to measure levels of intrinsic motivation and Motivation Capability. Analysis of the data clearly shows that 55% of overall employee commitment is derived from or influenced by extrinsic motivators (organizational vision, leadership, management practices, salary and benefits), while 45% is derived from or influenced by the individual's own intrinsic motivation factors and Motivation Capability.

Take a deep breath and let this information sink in. When you think that you are home and dry because you score high on employee satisfaction, you are actually only seeing 55% of the picture. Think of all the untapped potential just waiting to be mined. On the flip side, consider the rich talent you could lose at any moment due to lack of intrinsic motivation and individual Motivation Capability.

Until now, we've not had a good way to measure, develop and manage that individual aspect of motivation – the intrinsic motivation of individuals and their own personal capability to get and stay motivated and committed to their work. Yet, improving the capacity of every individual to be and stay resilient in the face of new roles, technology, structure and direction and to be and stay personally committed to meeting organizational objectives is critical to success.

Based on many years of experience we have identified these symptoms of people or organizations being low on extrinsic motivation, intrinsic motivation and Motivation Capabilities:

Symptoms of low motivation and engagement:

| | | |
|---|---|---|
| • Tendency to take the easy way out. <br> • Lack of sense of trust and fairness. <br> • Less flexibility and willingness to make an extra effort. | • "What's in it for me?" culture instead of a "How can I contribute?" culture. <br> • Low productivity due to boredom. <br> • Lack of enthusiasm for current projects or direction. | • "Silos" where work is carried out without regard for or integration with other parts of the organization. <br> • Lack of initiative, creativity or resourcefulness. <br> • Blaming others or outside circumstances for lack of progress. |
| Indicates deficiency in Extrinsic Motivation | Indicates deficiency in Intrinsic Motivation | Indicates deficiency in Motivation Capability |

The next few chapters will provide deeper insight into what our motivation factors are, how they work, and where you have much greater leverage than you may have realized in terms of identifying and managing motivation.

# Chapter 5: Managing Motivation

As I've outlined in the first few chapters, we know mass-motivation doesn't work. We know that both extrinsic rewards and an environment for intrinsic motivation are necessary; that personal engagement is individual and situational; and that the management of motivation requires dynamic - not static - initiative.

So how can you foster intrinsic motivation and build Motivation Capability in yourself and in any individuals you manage? Can it possibly (even easily!) be integrated as a natural part of your practice? Further, could you begin to shift this illusive responsibility for an individual's own intrinsic motivation and Motivation Capabilities from yourself to the people you manage? I have found that you can.

This requires a fundamental shift in our thinking:

| From: | To: |
|---|---|
| Mass motivation practices | Individual Motivation Capabilities |
| Manager-centric responsibility | Employee-centric responsibility |
| A laundry list of potential motivators | A personal and self-sustaining process |
| Scatter shot motivators | Custom tailored motivation actions |
| Static response to disengagement | Dynamic response to disengagement |

The underlying philosophy behind the Hierarchy of Motivation is that, in order to achieve lasting motivation, you must:

- Identify and act on the things that drain your energy

- Understand the impact of and assume responsibility for your Needs

- Actively apply and leverage your innate Talents

- Become Purpose-driven in your contributions, goals and choices

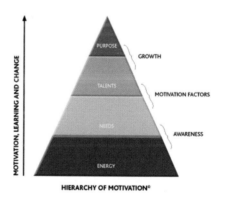

The Hierarchy of Motivation illustrates that the better you are at managing each level of the pyramid, the better you are at self-motivating, taking in new learning and managing yourself in a changing environment.

Without the skills to manage these functions, you are in danger of carving a path to frustration, stress, boredom and disengagement. Conversely, when you get rid of your Energy Drainers and your Needs are sufficiently addressed; you become oriented toward realizing your potential – in the form of using your Talents and living your Purpose.

Let's take a closer look at the Hierarchy of Motivation and see how it all ties together with Motivation Capabilities and intrinsic motivation.

The two lower levels – Energy and Needs - correspond to Motivation Capabilities – the extent to which your are able to identify what it takes to personally become and stay motivated, regardless of the presence of positive or negative external factors.

You can see the two lower levels of the Hierarchy as Energy and Needs. You can also look at the two lower levels as the foundation of a house. The stronger the foundation, the more you can build on top and the less it will be affected by storms, strong winds and earthquakes.

From cognitive psychology we know that the thoughts and meanings we assign to our experiences affect our emotions and, subsequently, our behavior. The more capable you are at responding to situations from a rational and objective perspective, the greater the chance that you will not be carried away by your emotions. I am not saying emotions aren't important. They are a valuable resource to you. However, the brain will fill in the blanks and make its own conclusions based on past experiences, rather than relate to the actual situation in an objective way.

Think of a situation when you were terribly wrong about your first impression of someone. That was caused by your brain's constant scanning for what is good and bad for you, making that initial assessment. If your brain makes the slightest connection with something negative from past experience, it makes a judgment. It could be that the person's expression looked like your father when he was angry, or the person's way of walking is just the same as a former boss whom you didn't like. The same brain areas involved in forming negative emotions and stress response (i.e. either fight or flight) are also involved in forming negative first impressions[5].

The lower your Motivation Capabilities, the greater is the possibility that when you experience chronic stress, you will be unable to distinguish real danger from reminiscence from past experience. The higher your Motivation Capabilities, the greater is the possibility that you are able to handle the situation from a non-judgmental and objective perspective. In Chapter 10, the neuroscience behind this is described in greater detail. With Motivational Capability, you say to yourself, okay I have a feeling of discomfort with this person but let's not be judgmental and let's see what happens.

The two upper levels in the Hierarchy of Motivation reflect intrinsic motivation – both neurologically and in terms of personal development. Brain research has shown that both psychological and physical health are positively affected when we use our innate Talents and when we contribute to something that is greater than ourselves[6]. Also, when you are aware of your Talents and passions and use them as a bridge for learning, the learning process is faster and more efficient[7]. Research also suggests that when you are driven by intrinsic motivation factors (Talents, passions and Purpose) you are able to remain more optimistic, even when things are not working the way you want them to[8].

Let's examine in detail the two lower levels in the Hierarchy of Motivation, which support Motivation Capability.

## Energy

Energy is the foundation of all activity - both mental and physical. It is therefore of great importance that we are able to identify and work to eliminate factors that drain our energy - those obstacles that we often, subconsciously, allow to steer our daily performance and long-term careers.

Research shows that 80% of that which drains our energy has to do with external factors such as other people's behavior, decisions made by others, or circumstantial limitations. Unfortunately, these factors are almost always beyond our control. Motivation, commitment and, ultimately, success rests on our ability to identify what is blocking our success, determine our ultimate goals, and generate options and possible actions. Take charge of the things we CAN control.

When Energy Drainers are left unaddressed, you might observe:

- Lack of initiative, creativity or resourcefulness
- Blaming of others or outside circumstances for lack of progress
- Performance problems or absenteeism
- Defensiveness
- Defeatist attitudes

## Needs

Our ability to recognize and respond to the Needs of others and ourselves is not only essential to motivation; it is also an important way to prevent stress. We are constantly confronted with things that threaten our Needs, and the more frequently our Needs are threatened, the higher the state of mental and interpersonal distress. Being in a long-term state of "threat" can bring about the condition we now recognize as burnout. The Needs level of the hierarchy represents our ability to be aware of, and responsible for, the impact of our personal Needs on the achievement of our goals.

When Needs are compromised, you might observe:

- Interpersonal conflicts

- Misalignment of goals and expectations within and across departments

- Frustration with, or lack of tolerance of, diverse ideas or approaches

- "Silos" where work is carried out without regard for, or integration with, other parts of the organization

- "Hallway conversations" – when communication or decisions are made outside of formal and open channels

Being aware of and being able to manage our Energy and Needs helps us to better understand and manage our behaviors and relationships. Much like finding and releasing the emergency brake on a car, we free ourselves from the friction and drag of Energy Drainers and threatened Needs and are able to become better resourced – from a neuropsychological standpoint - in our efforts to re-engage.

Motivation Capability is the competency of knowing and doing what it takes to remove obstacles and Energy Drainers and mitigate the impact of our personal Needs.

Now let's look at the two upper levels in the Hierarchy of Motivation which support Intrinsic Motivation.

## Talents

Our ability to learn, grow professionally and maintain long-term motivation depends on how effectively we leverage our personal Talents. Once we understand the value of utilizing our Talents and are actively applying them, our focus then naturally turns to facilitating and incorporating the Talents of others, which in turn boosts team productivity, innovation and

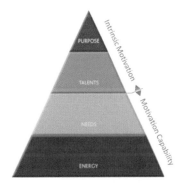

performance.

Organizations can generate much greater capacity and higher levels of commitment from individuals who more actively employ their personal Talents in their everyday life and work. The Talents level represents this ability.

When Talents are under-leveraged, you might observe:

- Disengagement or loss of top talent
- Requests for career development guidance or support
- Role confusion or "stepping on toes"
- Lack of enthusiasm for current projects or direction

## Purpose

Research shows that the goals that give people the greatest sustained energy and motivation are those that have personal meaning or are connected to a larger Purpose. The Purpose level addresses the extent to which you feel connected to, or receive meaning from, your work.

When Purpose is unclear, you might observe:

- Lack of a sense of community or camaraderie
- Progressively less passion for work or organizational direction
- Lack of connection to customer/stakeholders
- A "what's in it for me?" culture

Tapping into your Talents and being clear about the Purpose in your work is where growth, learning and real change occur. These levels are where our motivation lives.

When you consider the vast differences across people's personal Needs (financial, social, status-related, level of independence, etc.) and the incredible variety of Talents present in your teams (attention to detail, communication, creativity, strategic thinking, etc.) you can see how complex the question of motivation can be.

For instance, consider an organization that needs to change strategic direction. Its leaders have spent time hammering out the new strategy and are ready to communicate.  The tone is one of excitement and challenge and management enthusiastically call "all hands on deck!", "embrace change!", "think positively!"

Depending on where each individual is on the Hierarchy of Motivation, there will be any number of reactions.  There will be some percentage of the employee population that is energized and excited about the prospect of change.   Others will be downright hostile.   And a large number will be somewhere in the middle with very specific and unique questions, concerns, hopes and desires related to the new initiative.

As I have emphasized, motivation is individual and situational. Each of us is constantly moving up and down in the hierarchy of motivation as we cope with changing life circumstances. There will always be Energy Drainers in our lives; one thing or another will always threaten our Needs. We may feel blocked from developing and fine-tuning our Talents. We will on occasion lose perspective about what our personal contribution is to our work, as it is so easy to get caught up with day-to-day issues.

Using the Hierarchy of Motivation to identify and manage your own M Factor will allow you, as a manager, to respond to challenges and changes and quickly regain motivation for yourself when necessary.  It will also allow you to facilitate others in their quest to find and maintain their own M Factor.

Managing motivation is about the capacity to recognize – and even anticipate - disengagement and de-motivation.  It is about applying Needs and Talents to preempt or reverse the course of disengagement. And it is about being accountable for maintaining personal motivation over the long term.

The result? Increased motivation, productivity and efficiency, reduced stress and greater happiness. In the following chapters, we will take a look at each level of the Hierarchy of motivation in detail. For each level – Energy, Needs, Talents and Purpose - I will describe the symptoms, present the research behind the level, and provide an exercise for exploring that level for yourself and your staff.

# Chapter 6: The Impact of Energy

In this chapter we explore Energy, the first level of the hierarchy of motivation.   Our energy level provides the basis for our ability to perform and function in all of our daily roles, be it as a manager, colleague, spouse, or a parent. Unlike a car with a gas gauge, we do not have an indicator that warns us that we are tapping into our last reserves. In fact, we are very poor at realizing it when we are running out of energy.

If you think of the amount of energy you possess as being a finite or limited resource, it is easy to see how we can run out or feel overextended if too many tasks are all vying for a portion.  Over the long term, overextension of energy has detrimental effects on our cognitive abilities and general health by increasing our irritability, causing sleep problems, causing us to feel overwhelmed, guilty, and dissatisfied[9,10]. To an organization, the consequences of an overextended workforce include low morale, unmotivated employees, lack of initiative or creativity, and an inability to spot opportunities.

Deciding on which tasks to focus our energy and, more importantly, limiting the effects of inefficient tasks that waste energy is vital for individuals and corporations alike.  In the Motivation Factor framework,

Energy Drainers are any issues, whether internal or external, that impede progress or drag an individual or organization down. This chapter will guide you in identifying Energy Drainers and introduce a framework to use for minimizing or eliminating their effects.

## Identifying Energy Drainers

Think about any goal or objective – whether it is starting a new project, meeting your revenue target or installing a new technology. You can get excited about the prospect of achieving that goal, and yet a nanosecond later, you think, "Ugh! The reality of reaching this goal seems impossible with all the obstacles I have to tackle!"

By the time you consider all things in your way, you can't even SEE your goal, never mind achieve it! Energy Drainers whittle away at our patience, grind us down and leave us with a bigger mountain to climb than the one we started with. They take away our motivation.

This donkey is a very good picture of how someone who has too many Energy Drainers feels. It wouldn't matter if you were to give this poor donkey a carrot or a whack with a stick; it would not be going anywhere.

Once at capacity, you are compromised in your cognitive ability to perform tasks such as taking in new information or thinking creatively[10].

It may be tempting to just ignore the Energy Drainers and push through. Many of us do this on a regular basis, just to make it through the day. In fact, one of our workshop participants saw this picture and said, "Oh, that's no problem, just put some packages on the donkey's head and he'll balance right out!" In our frenetic, fast-paced, competitive working world, it is easy to go down that path.

Pushing forward without addressing and defusing Energy Drainers is like speeding down the highway with your emergency brake pulled. Even a Ferrari would quickly break in that situation. As a consequence of pushing forward, when people have reached their limit of Energy Drainers, they burn out, succumb to stress or start looking for a new job.

While an organization may be challenged by morale or motivation problems, it is important to recognize that each individual has unique Energy Drainers. Take for example the following Energy Drainers:

"I can't sell because I don't have the right brochures."

"I can't send the link to the customer because marketing hasn't created the copy"

"The guy in finance says we have to re-work the budget"

"I'm going to miss the deadline because production just changed the specs"

"Our meetings are unproductive because no one arrives on time"

"This project is going to fail because the other departments aren't committed"

"No, I didn't get that done, because I didn't hear back from the vendor"

"My star employee is frustrated with the constantly changing strategy"

A common theme among the example statements is that they lay blame on other people. In fact, our research has shown that 80% of that which drains people's energy has to do with other people or circumstances they can't directly influence. We often find ourselves dealing with others who we consider uncompromising and uncooperative, or we struggle with other circumstances that are beyond our control, leaving us with the feeling that we cannot influence the situation, that we are powerless.

The challenge is for us to engage our own powers to come up with new options for taking back the energy these situations demand from us. To be able to do that, we have to shift focus to what we can influence instead of what we cannot influence. A first step towards accomplishing this challenge is to understand the types of Energy Drainers and how they impact the individual.

## The four categories of Energy Drainers

Our research into Energy Drainers has found that there are four distinct categories:

1.  Expectation Energy Drainers
2.  Toleration Energy Drainers
3.  Boundary Energy Drainers
4.  Could/should/would Energy Drainers

In the following sections we will investigate each category in turn.

## Expectation Energy Drainers

An expectation arises when we assume that something will happen in a certain way. Our expectations concern what we expect from others and what we expect of ourselves. Consciously or unconsciously, we always have expectations of our surroundings and ourselves. The following is an example of how expectations can lead to a drain of energy for all involved in this common workplace situation.

*An employee (John) can have an expectation that his manager is responsible for motivating him. So every time he and the manager interact, John is just waiting for something to happen that can keep his motivation alive (reactive focus). The manager, on the other hand, is convinced that it should be motivation enough that John gets paid a high salary. As the end result, it becomes an Energy Drainer for both of them.*

The greatest negative consequence of expectation Energy Drainers is that we judge others when they don't live up to our expectations. We label them incompetent, selfish, mean, etc.     It is important to understand the dynamics of the labels we give to others and what those labels do to us.

For instance, how motivating is it to work for a manager whom we consider incompetent? How committed are we to a team if we consider the other team members to be disengaged?  In reality, no one goes to work every day thinking, "Yes, today I am going to be incompetent" or "What a great day to be disengaged".  To let go of judgment, we need to believe that everyone does the best they can with the abilities they have.

Tacit or unspoken expectations, the ones we kind of expect others to "just know", make up a substantial portion of our "mass of expectations". Generally speaking, we do not spend a lot of time communicating our expectations, because we tend to expect others to recognize and respond to what we need. Almost everyone has had the expectation that the boss will acknowledge that we are overworked, our spouse will notice when we require extra care and attention, our children will empty the dishwasher, or a colleague will understand that we need help.

Very often, all it takes to have our expectations met is to let the other people know what they are, that is make them explicit.  Indeed, this is the first step we advise to lessen or get rid of expectation Energy Drainers!

An expectation becomes a promise, once the other person agrees to do what you have asked of them. From that moment on, you are fully entitled to expect that it will be done. Of course, we sometimes find that even promises are broken:

- Something you were promised when you were hired was not delivered as promised
- Your colleagues don't keep the deadlines they have committed to
- You don't receive the information you have been promised
- The dishwasher is not emptied after all

The first step on the road to getting our expectations met is to make sure that they are clearly communicated. We have a tendency to believe that other people are mind readers. We kind of expect others to "just know" what we expect at any given time, and that their focus is the same as ours. But even if expectations are clearly communi-cated, we are faced with the fact that some of them may not be fulfilled.

## Boundary Energy Drainers

Setting boundaries is the next category of Energy Drainers we will focus on. If we take a stroll in the suburbs, we will see that physical boundaries are clearly marked by hedges, fences or walls. Boundaries are evident, and it is clear when we trespass on other people's territory. Unfortunately, personal boundaries are not like that. We are forced to communicate our personal boundaries. Recognizing and articulating our personal boundaries is extremely important. When we do so, we exhibit self-respect and a responsibility towards protecting our interests and ourselves.

To set a boundary is to make clear what we find acceptable or unacceptable. This could be related to personal space, commitment of time, sharing of personal information or other interests. Of course, having and communicating boundaries does not mean that others will change their behavior.

Though our boundary setting <u>might</u> motivate another person to change his or her behavior, we must remember that it is impossible to force change on others. As we mentioned earlier, many people struggle with this fact every day.

It can be difficult to set boundaries, because doing so is associated with fear that we might:

- Hurt someone else's feelings
- Be abandoned or isolated
- Make someone angry
- Be considered a bad or selfish person
- Develop a guilty conscience
- Not be loved
- Feel that we are to blame
- Owe a debt

Our sense of duty is often to blame for our inability to set boundaries: the idea that if we receive something, we must owe a debt of return. What do we owe our colleagues? Or what do we owe others who have been kind to us? What is reasonable, and what is not?

Many people solve this dilemma by avoiding to set boundaries on people to whom they feel obligated. In this way they avoid the guilt that follows from rejecting someone who has been kind to them – or to whom they would like to be kind.

Indeed, before we set a boundary, it is extremely important to decide whether we are willing to face the consequences. Boundaries without consequences are not boundaries. Take this scenario, for instance:

*At a large company, the changing nature of the business led the CEO to put pressure on several groups to be available around the clock, where they had previously worked regular hours five days a week. For one manager, this request pushed right up against his boundaries: he had already taken his group through salary cuts and several rounds of layoffs, which meant that the remaining staff was emotionally frayed and carrying much heavier workloads than ever before. He knew that they were close to the breaking point, and so he resisted the pressure.*

Taking a stand on boundary issues can sometimes come at a personal cost, which is why they are a particularly stressful Energy Drainer. Alternatively, not setting boundaries can lead to burnout and pent-up anger worse than the professional or social rejection you are afraid of when you do set a firm boundary.

A core principle in handling boundary Energy Drainers is the recognition and communication of your own boundaries. Recognize other people's feelings, but make it clear that your feelings warrant the same consideration. Each individual is responsible for owning and articulating their own reactions. Luckily, once the initial anger or defensiveness has subsided, the end result is often positive.

## Toleration Energy Drainers

Tolerations are all those things we put up with, but which are annoying or distracting. They are often temporary or short-lived and we don't find them "irritating" enough to actually deal with them. Toleration Energy Drainers make many people feel fatigued. Some examples of toleration Energy Drainers are: A negative person monopolizing a conversation, tons of email needing archiving, a wall that needs a coat of paint, or a colleague who is always badmouthing others.

The way to deal with these toleration Energy Drainers is to make sure you are aware of them. You might do this by grabbing a notebook and pen and "taking a stroll through your life". Each time you stumble on something that is not the way you would prefer it, you write it down. You don't need to find a solution right now; just writing it down is an effective process in itself.

Once you are aware of your toleration Energy Drainers, the next step is to decide for each one whether you want to take action or whether you want to make a conscious decision not to do anything. Often, a large Energy Drainer might be identified that takes several minor drainers away with it.

As a personal example, years ago I found that many of my tolerations involved the 1903 patrician villa that my husband and I lived in. There were a number of outwardly visible things that needed to be done: the base of the house needed rebuilding, the bathroom was due for renovation, and the fences needed repairing. On top of this, there was the everyday maintenance. Practically all of our spare time was dedicated to refurbishment.

We started the process by writing down all the things we felt should be changed, repaired, discarded, renovated, etc. We realized that if we were set on doing it all, it would be a time consuming and expensive process. Together, we came up with the following options for going forward:

- We could reduce the number of projects
- We could pay to get all the remaining things done
- We could work on the projects in the evenings
- We could sell and buy a newer house, which did not require as much maintenance

After long and difficult deliberations, we decided to sell and move to a newer house. It is one of the best decisions we have ever made. It released a whole lot of energy and freed up resources to do other things. It hugely improved the quality of our lives.

# Would, Should and Could Energy Drainers

The fourth category of Energy Drainers is "would, should, and could". All sentences beginning with "I could" or "I should" are usually associated with a guilty conscience.

Here are some typical examples:

- I <u>would</u> exercise more

- I <u>could</u> make a to do list

- I <u>should</u> be a better manager

The issue with would, should or could Energy Drainers is that the words are not action-oriented. If we substitute those words for "will", the sentences have an entirely different meaning.

- I will exercise more

- I will not make a to do list

- I will be better manager

Now that some of the sentences have been changed to "will", hence becoming action-oriented, it is vital to set concrete goals. Each time you attain a goal, your energy will be replenished, and your faith in possibility will be confirmed. Unfortunately, many of our intentions are what we call unquantifiable; goals that cannot be measured. Let us look again at an example from above: "I will exercise more". Exactly how often is that?

- Half an hour a week?

- Once a month?

- 4 times a year?

It is essential that our goals are quantifiable, for how else would we know when we have achieved them? For every goal, be specific about what is to be done, how often and by when.

# Working with Energy Drainers

This section will outline the Motivation Factor approach to working with Energy Drainers. There are five steps in this method, and exercises are included for each step. The method is intended to be conversational between two or more people, but it can work equally well if done individually. You are encouraged to try them out on yourself and colleagues.

## The 6 key steps in working with Energy Drainers

1.  Prepare the worksheet

2.  Define the Energy Drainers

3.  Uncover the Energy Drainers

4.  Define what you want instead, and what that would give you

5.  Generate options

6.  Defining action and deadlines

**1. Prepare the worksheet**

For this exercise you will need two worksheets. On the first worksheet, you list the Energy Drainers at the top and then outline four fields titled: Expectations, tolerations, could+would+should and boundaries.

| Energy Drainers | |
|---|---|
| 1. | |
| 2. | |
| 3. | |

| Expectations | Tolerations |
|---|---|
| | |
| Could, would, should | Boundaries |
| | |

On the second worksheet, you list what you want at the top and draw a vertical line down the middle of the paper. Title the left side "Options within your control" and the right side "Actions and deadlines".

| Want: | |
|---|---|
| Options within your control | Actions and deadlines |
| | |

## 2. Define the Energy Drainers

You actually WANT to explore them. This may seem counterintuitive, not to mention somewhat painful at first. After years of being told "be positive", "don't be so negative" and "look on the bright side", you invite the employee to vent, whine and rant about all the things that are wrong and in the way.

Research shows that putting words to the things that are threatening our success or well-being has significant positive effect on our ability to let go of those same things and move forward more freely. The idea is to give full voice to the things that are causing drag on your forward motion and then move onto constructive problem solving.

## 3. Uncover the Energy Drainers

The following conversation between a manager and a sales person is taken from a workshop on Energy Drainers. It is a good example of the types of responses people give and the types of probing questions the moderator should ask.

> Manager (M): What is in your way of being motivated and committed to achieving your target right now?

> Sales person (SP): I'm frustrated that:

> - Our prices are higher than our competitors' prices
> - I don't have up-to-date brochures
> - Our strategy keeps changing

> **Expectations**

> M: What are your expectations?

> SP: I would expect us to be competitively priced or have good clear reasons for being more expensive. I expect marketing to give us accurate information. And I expect not to have to keep apologizing to customers for a change in our direction

> **Tolerations**

> M: What are you tolerating as a result of these obstacles?

> SP: I'm reduced to negotiating on price with customers; I hate haggling. I delay communications to customers

because I don't have the right materials, and I'm embarrassed to have to go back on my word when our strategy changes.

## Boundaries

M: Does this cross your boundaries?

SP: Yes it does. I feel that I can't be at my best when I don't have the information and materials I need. And it affects my professional image when I have to go back and tell them that what I said last time has changed.

## Would, Could or Should

M: Is there anything you feel like you could have, should have or would have done to this point?

SP: No. I'm doing everything I can.

M: Is anything else bothering you about this?

SP: YES! I hate not being prepared, and I hate being going back on my word!

Your challenge as a manager (moderator) is to reserve judgment during these conversations. The point, indeed the necessity, here is to uncover the things that are affecting your staff's motivation. It's like lifting a loose shingle on your house and finding a nest of termites.

You wish they weren't there of course, but it doesn't help anyone to simply nail the shingle back on and think positively. Remember that Energy Drainers are very real to the person experiencing them, and they are inherently valid in that they cause a drag on motivation.

## 4. Define what you want instead of the Energy Drainer and what would that give you

It is important to remember here that the answer to this question must be something that is within our control. We want to focus on the things we CAN do as opposed to the things we cannot.

> M: What would you like instead of the Energy Drainer?

> S: I would like marketing to give me accurate materials, and I would like the strategy to stay the same for a few months at a time at least.

> M: If you had those things, what would they give you? (This is a good question to ask if the initial "want" is something that the person does not have direct control over).

> S: It would give me the ability to make a sale!

> M: So, ultimately, you want to make a sale?

> S: Of course! Many sales if I can help it.

Now we have shifted from what we don't want (inaccurate brochures, changing strategy, disadvantaged negotiations) to what we do want (many sales). We now are beginning to form an idea of a more ideal future.

## 5. Generate options

Energy Drainers take away motivation, largely because we see ourselves as powerless against them, dependent on the actions (or inactions) of others. The moment we see options and feel we have a choice, a shift occurs in the brain. We begin to see opportunities instead of obstacles.

Having identified the ultimate desire with the previous question, you can engage in a brainstorming exercise to list all the potential options available to achieve it. The more options the better, but we encourage listing three or more. Listing only one choice is not a choice at all. Listing two choices becomes a dilemma. Having three or more options gives us the feeling of having a genuine range of options.

> M: What options do have available to achieve sales?

> SP: Well, I could...

- Wait until marketing gets their act together
- Not talk about strategy
- Not use brochures at all
- Tell prospects that our strategy is flexible to respond to the market
- Focus on our value proposition ...

> M: I see some additional ideas. You could:

- Ask the prospect for what they need and create a custom response
- Calculate a ROI together with the prospect
- Invite me to visit the prospect to address questions of strategy

Once you have listed your options, you will feel action-oriented. Listing "crazy" (but technically possible) options also provides a benefit.

## 6. Define actions and deadlines

No matter which option you choose, it will be your choice – a conscious choice. Staying focused only on the things **you can do something about** and letting go of whatever is beyond your influence, restores power and opportunity to you.

Now, choose one or more items from the list of options that can be turned into actions. You can then guide the employee to identify:

- What will they do?
- With whom?
- By when?

This conversational exercise helps you use positive thinking to innovate ideas, encourage optimism through options, and establish forward movement through action.

The following are two examples taken from a Motivation Factor workshop, in which the team goal was to "work together to launch a new product". Below you see an example of two of the team members' Energy Drainers.

## Team member 1

1. What is your Energy Drainer in regard to working with the team to launch this new product?

| Energy Drainer |
| --- |
| I don't want to put in too much effort without getting back the same amount. I tend to do a lot more than the other team members. |

2. Uncovering the Energy Drainer

| Expectations | Tolerations |
|---|---|
| - I expect others to take things seriously and invest the same time and energy as I do<br>- I expect others to have the same need or urgency as I do to get things done<br>- I expect us to get some synergy out of this team | - I tolerate a low level of participation from others<br>- I tolerate that I get frustrated<br>- I tolerate that I am too forgiving |

| Could, would, should | Boundaries |
|---|---|
| - I should be more demanding<br>- I should be clearer to others/ myself about expectations | - I feel my standards for loyalty are compromised |

3. What do you want instead, and what would that give you?

4. Generate options that are within your control

5. Defining action and deadline

| I want to have the feeling that I am not the only one who is doing everything/all the things. That would make me less stressed. ||
|---|---|
| **Options** | **Actions** |
| Clarity about expectations | Make clear agreements about mutual expectations (alignment) (By March 1) |
| Be clear about what I want to do | |
| Create openness about who can do what | Think about how I see my contribution to the team |

| Options | Actions |
|---|---|
| Clear/open communication with mutual trust | Share my concerns based on previous experience |
| Share previous expectations | |
| Set boundaries/say no | |
| Help set scope | |

In this example, the team member chose to act on "Make clear agreements about mutual expectations (alignment)" and also set a deadline: March 1.

## Team member 2

1. What is your Energy Drainer in regard to working with the team to launch this new product?

| Energy Drainer |
|---|
| Lack of progress |

2. Uncovering the Energy Drainer

| Expectations | Tolerations |
|---|---|
| I expect progress | Lack of commitment |
| I expect people to keep promises | Missed deadlines |
| I expect others to be committed | |

| Could, would, should | Boundaries |
|---|---|
| I should be better at getting people to do what I expect them to do | Others don't do what they promise |
| It should not be necessary for me to be the one to hold them accountable | |

3. What do you want instead, and what would that give you?
4. Generate options that are within your control
5. Defining action and deadline

| I want progress. It would make it easier for me to set and meet my deadlines. | |
|---|---|
| Options | Actions |
| Work more | |
| Do more assignments myself | |
| Accept that we have different perceptions of the term 'progress' | |
| Find out what would motivate them to work faster | 1. Ask what it will take to create more progress (April 28 at next team meeting) |
| More follow-up | 3. Schedule weekly follow-up meetings (April 28) |
| Getting expectations aligned | 2. Getting expectations aligned (April 28) |

Actively working with Energy Drainers helps you see how full your gas tank is, and what you might do proactively to keep your reserves up. You can do this for yourself using the prompts in the exercise. Many people start the day off with these exercises in an effort to clear the path to a productive, self-directed day. Others use it when they feel overwhelmed or "stuck". In any case, it is a useful tool to use as a manager with your staff members and your team as a whole. By incorporating it into ad-hoc, one-on-one and team meetings, you develop the team's capacity – in real time - to proactively manage the factors that impact its effectiveness.

## Chapter summary

In this chapter, the concept of Energy Drainers was introduced, along with the importance of being able to recognize them and how they affect our lives. Equally important is being able to do something about them. The Motivation Factor framework has five steps to help identify them, categorize them, generate options to get rid of them, and finally define actions for the future. For more information on the neuroscience behind the framework, see Chapter 10.

By following the framework steps, either alone or in a group, you will clear your mind, allowing you to focus on more important issues or tasks. It is our belief that controlling the effects of Energy Drainers is a major step towards better health and cognitive happiness.

# Chapter 7: The Nature of Needs

In this chapter we explore Needs, the second level of the hierarchy of motivation. It is commonly known that all human beings have similar basic Needs such as health, safety and belonging. The concept of Needs is well described in Abraham Maslow's hierarchy of needs[1,2]. In addition to basic needs, every individual has a set of more nuanced personal Needs. It is these Needs that are most influential in guiding personal responses to everyday events and motivation.

Our ability to recognize and respond to our own and others' Needs is an important way to reduce stress and anxiety. In addition, understanding and managing our Needs further impacts our personal and interpersonal development. This is important for teams to enhance the productive collaboration of multiple people, all with their own set of Needs.

In the Motivation Factor framework, Needs are patterns of behavior that make us feel comfortable and safe. When one of our Needs is not met, we feel threatened and usually respond with a visceral or primitive emotion such as anger, fear, or even violence. Of course this stress response (fight or flight reaction) is appropriate when we are being attacked by a tiger, but not when a colleague is constantly interrupting us. Surprisingly, the same physiological response is triggered in the brain in both situations[11].

We are constantly confronted with things that threaten our Needs, and the more frequently our Needs are threatened, the higher the state of mental distress. This chapter will explain how the Motivation Factor framework determines individual Needs and then how to work with them to diminish visceral response, reduce stress, and enhance personal communication.

## Identifying your Needs

Try to remember an instance when you lost control after someone or something "pushed your buttons".  It is possible you reproached someone with a severity that you later realized was completely out of proportion to what happened. This is a classic example of a reaction to a Need not being met.  In these types of situations, you were threatened sufficiently to evoke a fight or flight response, thereby invoking the stress response[11].  Now, your reaction is governed by more primitive emotions and not rational well thought-out reasoning.

Indeed, our stress response is triggered when:

- We believe that our personal Needs will not be met
- Someone is preventing us from meeting our personal Needs, or
- We believe we have to fight to have our Needs met.

In a dysfunctional team setting, the following traits can be observed when interactions are governed by fight or flight reactions:

- Interpersonal conflicts
- Misalignment of goals and expectations within and across departments

- Frustration with, or lack of tolerance of, diverse ideas or approaches
- "Silos" where work is carried out without regard for or integration with other parts of the organization
- "Hallway conversations" — when communication or decisions are made outside of formal and open channels.

By understanding our own and others' Needs, we free our brain up to more effectively learn, grow and manage change. Once interactions are not governed by our primitive reactions, individually as well as in teams, relational understanding and openness to growth results in:

- Higher productivity
- Fewer conflicts
- Greater resilience
- Increased cognitive ability and capacity for innovation and growth

A powerful effect of not having our Needs met is our tendency to judge highly negatively the people we hold responsible. For example:

"The marketing manager is incompetent"

"The accounting department is lazy"

"My manager is a control freak"

"I'm the only one who does anything around here"

"That VP is a pompous jerk"

"I'm not working with her because she rude and disrespectful"

"No one appreciates my work"

"If they would follow the rules everything would work fine"

Sound familiar? It's a wonder how any of these incompetent, lazy, pompous, rude, rule breaking, disrespectful people GET jobs, never mind keep them! But are their characters that inherently flawed? Do they wake up each morning, stretch and greet the sunrise saying, "What a GREAT day! I can't wait to get to work and be uncooperative. I think I'll refuse to see the plain facts and maybe interrupt a few people while they try to make a point. Yeah...It's going to be a good one." I'll wager a guess that most don't.

So what makes them behave in ways that are unproductive, nonsensical and even damaging? The answer is that our own personal Needs have skewed the way we perceive others. When our personal Needs are threatened, we blame and judge.

Participants in Motivation Factor workshops have offered a wide variety of responses when asked what kind of behaviors they dislike the most in other people. Answers include selfishness, interrupting, arrogance, laziness, disrespect, rudeness, and making excuses. When asked to recall their reaction to the last encounter, typically one of three types of answers is given: 1) "I wanted to punch them in the nose" (fight) reaction, 2) "I disengage or withdraw" (flight) reaction, or 3) "I didn't know/ what to do" (freeze) reaction. None of these responses is conducive to effective interactions.

## Motivation Factor Indicator

It is hard for people to put into words what their personal Needs and Talents are. This is why we developed the Motivation Factor Indicator. If you haven't already completed the Motivation Factor Indicator, it is now time to do so.

Our research has shown that there are some 200 Needs and 170 Talents, which we have grouped into 14 broad categories of Needs and 9 broad categories of Talents.

As an example, the words supporting the Need main category of *Order* are: Perfection, Symmetry, Consistent, Sequential, Structure, Unvarying, Rightness, and Literalness.

This is why the Need *Order*, depending on the individual, can mean any of following:

- structure, process and guidelines
- physical alignment of objects
- chronological steps taken

Likewise, the Talent *Mastery* and the words supporting the Talent main category of *Mastery* are: Expert, Dominate field, Adept Superiority, Primacy Preeminence, Greatest, Best, Outdo, Set standards, Excellence.

This is why the talent *Mastery*, depending on the individual, can mean any of following:

- to be the expert in a given area
- to know every detail
- to set new standards within a field of interest

You can read more about the Motivation Factor Indicator and the research behind it on our website www.motivationfactor.com.

Here, as an example, are my Top 3 Needs:

**Freedom**

The need for freedom can mean that independence fuels you. You are likely most comfortable when you have a high degree of influence on how you use your time and a choice of which tasks to work on. You may feel constrained by rules and limitations. | The day is my own. | Self-management. | Lots of options. | Freedom to choose.

**Personal power**

The need for personal power can mean that you want to make an impact. Being able to influence your circumstances is most likely crucial for you. You may dislike apathy and be frustrated by "victims" of circumstance. | Opinion counts. | Seek to Inspire. | Authority and Impact. | Bringing Know how.

**Balance**

The need for balance can mean that you will tend to strive for equality in many situations. It may be balance in your personal or professional life, but it can also be balance in work assignments, conversations or relationships. You may feel uncomfortable in situations when attention is not being paid equally. | Counterweight and compensation. | Stabilize and counterbalance. | Consensus and harmony. | Holistic approach to tasks.

My Need for personal power is met through my speaking and working with individuals and organizations. My Need for balance is satisfied by maintaining a focus on being a good role model and by setting aside half an hour for reflection every day. My Need for freedom is met through my understanding that I **always** have options and that **my** life is guided by **my** choices.

## Understanding your Needs

Once you know your personal Needs, you are much more capable of seeing a situation for what it is, managing your stress reaction and responding productively. Moreover, you can learn to compare your mental dialogue with the actual situation you are in. You can learn to tell the difference between what you can change and what you cannot. In essence, you can learn how to master your mental processes rather than being at their mercy.

Each of us, either consciously or subconsciously, establishes "rules" to determine whether our Needs are being satisfied. It is important to uncover those rules in order to become aware of, and discover ways to better manage, the interplay between Needs and behavior.

It is central to our work in the Needs workshop to find out where in life one's Needs are not being fulfilled, and what consequence there might be. For example, a person who does not feel respected by his spouse may increasingly seek to have his Need for respect fulfilled at work. A person with a strong Need for security may often seek work in a place where job security is a priority. A person who does not feel accepted at work may tend to seek acceptance outside of work, etc.

The following two examples will show how the same situation can be viewed quite differently, once personal Needs are known and taken into account.

**Example 1:**

My husband, 14-year-old daughter, 16-year-old son and I took the Indicator assessment, and our resulting Top Five Needs are shown in Figure 1.

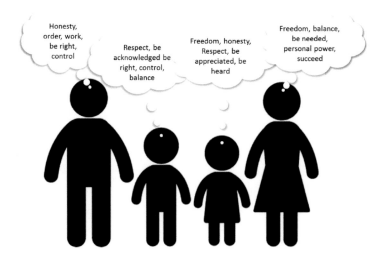

*Figure 1: Top 5 Needs of my family members*

This situation is a typical example of what would happen when my husband went into my daughter's room, seeing piles of clothes everywhere, clean and dirty clothes in one big mess. Their dialogue would usually go something like this:

My husband: "Why didn't you clean up your room as you promised it half an hour ago?"

My daughter: "I will do it in a minute"

My husband: "You said that half an hour ago"

My daughter: "I said I will do it in a minute"

My husband: "You said that half an hour ago also, so I want you to do it right now!"

My daughter: "This is my room and I decide when to clean it! You can just close the door"

By looking at my husband's and daughter's Needs in Fig. 1, the reasons for their escalating and unproductive conversation become clear. My husband's Need for 'order' is definitely not being meet, nor is his Need for 'honesty'. So he tries to make her agree that he is right and that she has been dishonest. He also tries to 'control' the situation by demanding the mess be cleaned "right now".

On the other hand, my daughter wants the 'freedom' to do what she wants without him interfering. She tries to get the message through by shouting louder and louder in an attempt to be 'heard'. Besides she is really not feeling 'respected', and she is definitely not 'being appreciated'.

If you take a look at my Needs you might understand why I am not angered the same way as my husband. I don't have a Need for 'order' (not that I don't like a clean house) but my 'freedom' is more important to me, so I am actually on her side in this situation. So I try to create some 'balance' by stepping in as the negotiator and by doing that, my Need for 'being needed' is met.

**Example 2:**

Let's say that you are a trusting person, full of ideas, and you love to try new things. You have a boss who encourages you and provides you with a high degree of freedom to try out your ideas. Your boss is always inviting you to present your ideas at the company board meetings.

One day, you get a new boss with a totally different approach. Every time you put a new idea out there, he starts to challenge you, and all he sees are the holes in the cheese. He wants to present ideas himself at the board meetings.

After completing the Motivation Factor Indicator, you learn that your top 3 personal Needs are honesty, to succeed, and be appreciated. Your new boss is threatening your need for 'honesty' when he challenges your ideas because he does not think that you have taking everything into account. Furthermore, you are not felling 'successful' or 'appreciated' by his negative approach and by him wanting to present your ideas at the board meetings. He is not only threatening your Needs, he also stands in your way of getting them met.

Now let us assume that the new manager's top 3 personal Needs are certainty, control and order. In his last job, he was used to being criticized if he didn't have control of every little detail. Especially when presenting at board meeting, he would be met with suspicion. All this was the reason for him applying for a new job. He promised himself that when he got the new job, he would make sure that his employees would not have to go through the same thing. Therefore, he wants to make sure that every aspect has been taken into consideration, if any criticism should come up. He also decided to do the presentations at board meetings himself to spare the employees from being put on the spot.

He senses that you are bit hostile, but he just does not get it. He is only trying to protect you.

While these two example Needs conflicts may seem extreme, there is constant potential for conflict in all of our relationships with spouses, children, friends, colleagues, and bosses. The thing with Needs is that we naturally believe other people have the same Needs as we do. However this is not the case. Everyone has different Needs.

Even without completing the Motivation Factor Indicator, it is possible to determine what some of your personal Needs are by simply thinking of the characteristics of a great manager or mentor you admire.

If you have a Need for freedom you might say "she was a great manager because she made me find my own way of doing things". Or you might say "she was a great manager because she always gave me clear instructions as to how she wanted me to solve the assignment" – that is if you have a Need for order.

If you personally hate to be given instructions because that takes away your freedom – then of course you won't do that to other people. We manage from what works for us. Therefore learning your own Needs and leaning the Needs of your employees is not only key to your success, but also a key factor in preventing stress.

# Working with Needs

This section will outline the Motivation Factor approach to working with Needs. There are six steps in this method, and exercises are included for each step. The method is intended to be conversational between two or more people, but it can work equally well if done individually.

## The 6 key steps in working with Needs

1. Prepare the worksheet

2. Uncover the 5 behaviors you dislike the most in other people

3. Uncover your Top 5 Needs from the Indicator and how you interpret each Need

4. Link your dislikes to your Needs

5. Link a Need to a behavior you dislike

6. Uncover what others may dislike, given my Needs

## 1.  Prepare the worksheet

Draw a vertical line down the middle of a paper, title the left side "5 behaviors I dislike in others" and the right side "My Top 5 Needs".

| 5 behaviors I dislike in others | My Top 5 Needs |
|---|---|
|  |  |
|  |  |
|  |  |
|  |  |
|  |  |

1) Ask: "Consider a person who displays one of the disliked behaviors. Which Need might that person have that would compel them to behave in such a way?"

2) Ask: "Given your Needs, what behavior might you exhibit that others might dislike?

## 2. Uncover the 5 behaviors most disliked

Think of the most annoying behaviors of other people that you dislike. Think about situations when you saw this behaviour unfold.

## 3. Uncover your Top 5 Needs from the Indicator

On the right column of the worksheet, write your 5 Needs from the Indicator. Think about how you interpret each need and think of situations when you saw this Need unfold.

## 4. Link your dislikes to your Needs

This is an important step when working with your Needs. For each of your disliked behaviors in turn, ask yourself which of my Needs is threatened by that behaviour?  For example, if you don't like dishonesty, it would not be surprising if you have a Need for honesty and it is being threatened. Draw a line connecting the dislike to any of your Needs that are being threatened.

## 5.   Link a Need to a behavior you dislike

Now that you are more aware of what your Needs are and how they can drive your behaviour, it is equally important to be aware of the Needs of others.   For each of your dislikes, ask yourself what need might a person have that would compel them to behave in such a way?

One commonly disliked behaviour is dishonesty. It can be very difficult to figure out what makes people dishonest. As an example:

*A sales representative has a Need to succeed and to be appreciated. The salesperson has a customer who will sign a contract here and now if he can be promised a one-month delivery time. From experience, the sales representative knows that this will be very difficult, but s/he can be heard saying that it can be done. The sales representative knows that if s/he displays any hesitation, the deal will not be signed. The sales representative's Need to succeed and to be appreciated once the contract signed is dominating his/her behaviour in this moment.*

## 6.   Uncover what others could dislike given your Needs

It is equally important to be aware of how your personal Needs may be disliked by others.   For each of your Needs ask yourself, what behavior might I exhibit that others might dislike?  Knowing how you might elicit a visceral response in someone else is vital.   Instead of managing people the way you would like to be managed, you can now manage them the way they would like to be managed.

The following are two examples taken from Motivation Factor workshops where participants are led through the steps in working with their Needs.

## EXAMPLE 1:

| 5 behaviors I dislike most in others | My top 5 needs: |
|---|---|
| Make other people feel small | Be heard |
| Selfish | Balance |
| Disrespect (discourteous, rude, not valuing) | Respect |
| Negative | Be appreciated |
| Dismissive | Honesty |

## EXAMPLE 2:

| 5 behaviors I dislike most in others | My top 5 Needs: |
|---|---|
| Disrespect | Freedom |
| Exploitation | Honesty |
| Untruthfulness | Balance |
| Fanaticism | Respect |
| Selfishness | Dutifulness |

## Chapter summary

In this chapter, the concept of Needs was introduced as well as the opportunity to determine your own Needs by using the Motivation Factor Indicator. With this knowledge comes not only awareness of why you react the way you do when your Needs are not met, but also awareness of why other people behave the way they do.

The Motivation Factor framework for this chapter reinforces your awareness by linking your dislikes of others to your Needs. Equally important is the appreciation for how your Needs could potentially be interpreted as dislikes by people around you.

For those interested, a neuroscientific rationale for the Framework is available in Chapter 10. By following these steps, either by yourself or in a group, you will learn to take responsibility to ensure that your Needs are met.

# Chapter 8: The Value of Talents

In this chapter we discuss Talents, one of the two upper levels in the Hierarchy of Motivation. These two levels - Talents and Purpose - correspond to Intrinsic Motivation – the extent to which your work is aligned with your inherent qualities, your passions and what you find meaningful.

Tapping into your Talents and being clear about the Purpose in your work is where growth, learning and real change occur. These levels are where the seed   of our true motivation lives. Our ability to learn, grow professionally and maintain long-term motivation depends on how effectively we leverage our personal talents.

Once we understand the value of utilizing our talents and are actively applying them, our focus then naturally turns to facilitating and incorporating the talents of others, which in turn boosts team productivity, innovation and performance. The Talents level represents this ability.

In my workshops on Personal Talents, I ask participants "What are you best at? What are the skills, qualities or 'knacks' you have that your family, friends and colleagues tend to remark on?"

Some of the responses from participants include:

"Communicating in a diplomatic way"

"Being creative"

"Thinking out of the box"

"Seeing the big picture and a path to get to the goal"

"I'm good at research and delving into details"

"I'm persistent"

"People say I'm an excellent listener"

"I have excellent intuition and can see connections where others don't"

Most everyone can identify at least one ability or inclination that tends to come naturally to him or her. Participants are then asked to recall the last time they were involved in that "best at" activity and describe how it felt to contribute in that way.

Some of the descriptions were:

"Empowered"

"Proud"

"Valued"

"Energizing"

"Like I had Purpose"

"Wanted to do more"

In short, it feels motivating. Try it now for yourself by recalling the last time things seemed to flow effortlessly across your desk. A time when you were super-motivated and everything just seemed to go well. This is exactly the effect we experience when we use our Talents. This is the essence of internal motivation.

We know the following four things about Talents:

1. **We have them**. Everyone can think of a Talent or natural ability that they are able to perform at a level that is above the norm. More formally, a Talent can be described as the possession and development of a skill, and the expression of a natural aptitude of a sensorimotor and/or cognitive skill[12]. Essentially, Talents shape the way we view and interact with the world around us. For example, some people have an inordinate amount of curiosity and want to understand everything (i.e. mastery), while others view the world more globally and see interactions (i.e. strategic). No one Talent is better than another; it is how Talents are used that is important for motivation.

2. **We feel good when we use them**. The way we feel when we use our Talents has been investigated since Aristotle and more recently in the field of positive psychology[13]. Briefly, what has been found is that using our Talents leads to greater happiness and an increased sense of well-being or eudaimonia[14]. More information on this line of research can be found in Chapter 10. In addition, when we use our natural Talents, we contribute to a feeling of effortlessness and "flow": the ideal balance of challenge and skill; effortlessness without being boring.

3. **We can use them to learn more efficiently**. We learn by making new connections between areas and neurons in the brain[15]. This is called neural plasticity. Learning can also be faster if there are already connections in the brain that are related to the new information (i.e. it is easier to learn about a new camera if you are already familiar with many other types of camera)[16]. By leveraging our Talents, we give the brain a boost towards learning new skills. The brain areas involved in learning are negatively impacted by chromic stress especially the hormone cortisol[17]. People who are effectively using their Talents (i.e. greater eudaimonia) have lower levels of cortisol[18], suggesting that less stress is enabling the learning areas to function more efficiently.

4. **We can overuse them**.  Since Talents are ingrained, we can take them for granted.  They feel so natural to us, we may not even realize we are using them.  In fact, we can default to our Talents in ways that can get in our way if we are not paying attention.

In teams, the identification and coordinated application of Talents is a powerful and often untapped reserve. And like Needs, it is better to manage our Talents than to have our Talents manage us, or worse, simply languish.

## Leveraging Talents

Our ability to leverage our Talents to develop new competencies can be compared with the way we learn in school. When children start to learn arithmetic, we begin by showing them something recognizable. We ask them, how many apples do I have? Six apples? So if I remove two apples, how many are left?  If the child has learned to count it will be relatively easy to figure out that there are four apples left.  From there, we build on the child's familiarity with apples and counting to introduce and build skill in arithmetic.

Conversely, if we were to show the calculation 6-2=4, the child would not be able to recognize the symbols or understand what they represent. It would take significant effort to make the child understand, since the calculation consists of entirely unknown factors and nothing to build from.

The key to building on our talents is to put words to our "apples" so that we can more easily identify and apply them effectively to new situations. Take for example the case of the highly valued senior executive in one of the largest transportation companies in the world. Her aggressive and unprofessional treatment of colleagues and staff was threatening to derail her success. She had been to all the "people skills", communication and management courses available without success. Indeed, she did not have a talent for "Empathy".  Given that the brain learns fastest and most efficiently by beginning with what you already know, if a person is lacking a basis upon which to build an understanding of emotional intelligence, building emotional intelligence itself is going to be a monumental – perhaps even impossible – task.

Through coaching, it was discovered that while this executive did not have a natural talent in the area of Empathy, she did have a talent for Discovery. She interpreted Discovery as "being curious about things". Working with her, I asked if she might not direct that curiosity toward the people with whom she worked. Remember, that simply by engaging in discussion about your Talents, you are engaging those areas in the brain and triggering the release of happy hormones. Suddenly, for the first time, development seems POSSIBLE. There is immediate recognition of the known Talent and subsequent connections being formed toward the desired new competency. By putting her Talent for Discovery into play, the executive was able to develop and demonstrate an interest in others, which significantly improved her work performance and relationships.

You can build new competencies more efficiently and with more confidence when you draw upon your existing talents. By using something recognizable as a starting point – a Talent for "Discovery", for instance, where you already have a close set of connections - you can build a bridge to form new connections.

## Overusing Talents

To a great extent, working with Talents is a matter of helping people put their Talents into play, but it is equally important to find out if they are overusing their Talents. If a team member has a Talent for "empathy" and overuses this Talent, he/she might find it uncomfortable to initiate "difficult" conversations or be limited by sensitivity to the reactions of others. A team member with a Talent of "mastery" might find it difficult to share responsibility, outsource things or delegate, because s/he has an inner urge to master the work alone, or s/he believes that other people will not be as good at it as s/he will be.

To one CFO, delegating work was a challenge. His primary Talent was "mastery", and he was naturally drawn to understanding and retaining responsibility for all parts of his function. Further complicating matters, his primary Need was "to be needed". No wonder delegation was difficult!

By identifying the Needs and Talents in play, he was able to clarify those work functions he found most draining and those he found most energizing. In his case, budgeting was quite satisfying whereas budget follow-up was not. This recognition led him to decide to master budgeting and outsource follow-up. He directed his Talent for "mastery" toward the area of greatest satisfaction for him and, at the same time, his Need "to be needed" was not threatened by this decision.

## Using Talents

By exploring and actively applying your primary Talents, you become more engaged and intrinsically motivated in both work and life. Moreover, once the value of utilizing your Talents is understood, your focus naturally turns to recognizing, incorporating and facilitating other people's Talents. Imagine managing staff to maximum Talent potential so that team members readily acknowledge and actively integrate each other's Talents toward the task at hand – regardless of function, level, or "turf". When Talents are used, true teamwork happens.

Living a Talent-based life is all about allowing Talents to be expressed in everything we do, and using them as a pathway to new learning.

There are, of course, many instances when you or your team members have tasks to accomplish that are less than motivating. Whether it is making a presentation, researching the causes of a challenging problem or analyzing the budget, there are some activities you just don't relish. Leveraging your Talents is one way to get re-committed and focused on the task at hand. Consider this example from my own experience.

Many salespeople hate cold-calling someone they have never spoken with before to set up a meeting to tell them more about the product they want to sell. A lot of people get annoyed when they are contacted in this way, often because they are and have already been interrupted by five other sales calls that morning. The salesperson is often turned down and, as a rule of thumb, only one out of ten people agrees to see you.

Back in my sales days, I experienced what it meant to leverage my own Talents to become more committed and motivated towards this challenging activity. Looking back at it, I realized that the times when I actually enjoyed cold-calling was when I used my Talents of "catalyze", "creativity" and "discover" during the process.

### 1) Catalyze

Catalyze can mean that you have a natural ability to make things happen and you induce other people to take action. You may love to set new initiatives in motion and are always on the lookout for new exciting things to do. | Kick-start new initiatives. | Setting new ships to sea. | Proactive and impatient. | Entrepreneurial approach.

### 2) Creativity

Creativity can mean that you tend to look at things differently, see possibilities and are on the lookout for the "new". Building something out of nothing, whether a new product or a new way of doing things, most likely fascinates you. | Induce new initiatives. | Leave no stone unturned. | Innovative and productive. | Create.

### 3) Discover

Discover can mean that you tend to uncover things never seen before or have a curiosity about new concepts or opportunities. Research and "behind the scenes" information may be especially appealing. | Context in new ways. | Actively inventing new things. | Understanding interpreting. | Develop and explore.

First, I made up a list of all the advantages I believed the customer would get by purchasing our solutions.    Then I developed a questionnaire based on these advantages, but rephrased in terms of Needs, e.g.: 'Is it important to your company that all your customer data is located in one place?'  Finally, I called the customer and said we were doing a survey about the maintenance of customer data and would they answer a few questions. They usually would and, as I moved through the questionnaire, I got their attention and was invited to meet with them. I was extremely motivated because I was internally driven through the entire process.

From preparation through the meeting itself I used all my Talents, as you can see:

- Developing the list of benefits required me to learn how the products were distinct in the market (discover, creativity)
- Developing the questionnaire (discover, creativity)
- Obtaining information about the customer's situation (catalyze, discover)

Today, I live my life in a Talent-based way to an even larger extent, because I have developed my entire business based on my Talents. When I develop new programs and presentations, I use all my Talents. When I seek new knowledge, I use my Talent 'discover'. During the learning process related to obtaining knowledge on a subject, my brain naturally looks for new connections and ways of perceiving things. I can sit for days totally immersed in the process. I don't need anyone to motivate me. I am 100% self-motivated.

# Working with Talents

This section will outline the Motivation Factor approach to working with Talents. There are seven steps in this method, and exercises are included for each step. The method is intended to be conversational between two or more people, but it can work equally well if done individually. You are encouraged to try them out on yourself and colleagues.

## The 7 key steps in working with Talents

1. Get feedback

2. Prepare worksheet

3. Uncover your 5 Talents from the Indicator and articulate how you interpret each Talent

4. Link your Talents to the feedback

5. Elaborate what you would gain from improving (what would that give you)

6. Bridging the Talents

7. What, who and when

## 1.  Get feedback

Ask 4 people who know you really well to give you feedback on:

> One thing that you do really well

One thing that you can improve

It is important that you tell people why you want their feedback (e.g. because I want to become a better manager, parent, or spouse). If you are asking for the feedback in a work context, you can benefit from asking your manager, 1 or 2 subordinates, and 1 or 2 peers to get a variety of perspectives.

If you don't want to use the feedback option, you can also do this part by giving yourself feedback. What in your own opinion are you doing really well, and what would you like to improve?

## 2.  Prepare the worksheet

The next thing you do is to divide a page into three columns and label the columns as in the table below.

| Talents | Improvements | What would that give me |
|---------|--------------|-------------------------|
| 1)      |              |                         |
| 2)      |              |                         |
| 3)      |              |                         |
| 4)      |              |                         |
| 5)      |              |                         |

## 3.  Articulate each Talent

On the left, write the 5 Talents from the Motivation Factor Indicator and briefly articulate how you interpret each Talent. You should think about how you use the Talent in your work and in your free time. Can you maybe use it even more? Or are you overusing the Talent? Does it give you energy?

## 4. Link your Talents to the feedback

When you look at the feedback and the things that people find that you do really well, how do you see your Talents reflected in this? Are there any surprises?

We usually don't give our Talents much attention because when something becomes natural to us we have a perception that "anyone" can do the same. Judgments about incompetence often originate from this perception. Look around and pay attention to what people say: She should have more empathy, or he should be more strategic or detail-oriented. Everyone has their unique way of using their Talents, and even people with same Talents can use them differently. Honor the feedback you get and let it sink in as "your" uniqueness and source for growth.

When you look at the feedback and the things you can improve, you should ask yourself what would be most impactful for you to change? (Write it in the middle column "improvements"). You need to be very "critical" here. Often these desired improvements turn up again and again from others.

I have coached hundreds of people, and my first question when it comes to improvements is always "has this come up before?" In a large majority of cases, the person has heard it before, but lacked the follow-through in order to make a change. Successful improvements can only happen if you find your own motivation for change. If you don't really see the benefits, you would likely fail to make the change, even with the best intentions at heart.

## 5. Elaborate what you gain from improving

You should write in the right column what you would gain from this improvement. Motivation is key here. When I ask this question in relation to feedback "what would you gain from this change" the person is often not able to answer. Or the answer is somewhat related to satisfying other people's Needs. Unfortunately, this reason is not good enough to motivate in the long term.

You have to **feel** an urge to make the change; it is not enough to rationalize what it would give. The better you are at mapping the fulfilment of your Talents and Needs to improvement, the more likely you will succeed. If you are not able to articulate and feel what you would gain, you should choose another "improvement" to work with.

## 6. Bridging the Talents

Next step is to find out how your Talents can support you in your improvements. In this example the participant made the following conclusion: "I have overused my Talents "mastery" and "contribute", because I just love details and I feel good when other people ask for my help. I will use my Talent "lead" to make some conscious choices about what it is critical for me to master and what is not. Using the "discover" and "catalyze" Talents will help me focus on finding and leveraging my team's Talents."

## 7. What, Who and when

Now that you have decided what to change, you should make some decisions about how to make it happen, what kind of support you need, and set deadlines for when you will do it. In this example the participant listed this:

| What I need to do | Who can support me | When will I do it |
| --- | --- | --- |
| Find out what is critical for me to master | My boss and my team | Right after this workshop |
| Leverage my team's Talents | HR and external coaches | I will meet with HR next week to get some ideas about what we can do and the budget |

## Example case

The following example is taken from Motivation Factor workshops where participants are led through the steps in working with their Talents.

| 5 Talents | Improvement | What would that give me? |
|---|---|---|
| Win | - Be more patient | It would decrease my level of stress and make me better at finding new ways to contribute to the team. |
| Communicate | - Be better at listening | |
| Discover | | |
| Connecting | | By training my listening skills and not be so impatient I would be able to make more meaningful and customized contribution and communication |
| Contribute | | |

In this example, the participant made the following conclusion: "I am overusing my Talents "communicate", "discover", and "contribute". I am so busy finding answers ("discover") that I interrupt people just to make them understand ("communicate") that I know what they are talking about and I have the right answer ("contribute"). I want to use my Talent "win" to help me support my improvements. I can use my Talent "discover" to be more curious about my own behaviour and about what people are telling me.

| What do I need to do? | Who can support me? | When will I do it? |
|---|---|---|
| Set new inspiring standards for listening that I can measure myself against | I can make a daily journal about my wins | Right away |
| Inform the team that I do want to improve my listening skills and patience. Agree on a sign when they feel I am not listening or I am too impatient | My employees and wife | Right away |
| Learn coaching skills | Other people who have completed coaching training. I will seek references for coaching training | I will find the budget to this in next financial year (begins in two months) |

# Chapter summary

In this chapter, the concept of Talents was introduced along with the importance of being able to recognize them and how they affect our lives. Not fully taking advantage of your Talents can lead to feeling bored, disengaged or unenthusiastic about your work.

These naturally occurring abilities, skills and qualities give us our intrinsic motivation. The Motivation Factor framework includes a seven-step workshop that helps to identify Talents, understand them in relation to what other people think of you, and work on personal improvement. More information on the neuroscience behind Talents is available in Chapter 10.

We must recognize our Talents and value, develop and apply them. This is where our biggest opportunity for development and motivation lies, as well as many beneficial effects on physical health.

# Chapter 9: The Power of Purpose

We now arrive at the fourth and final level of the Hierarchy of Motivation. Purpose is the second of the two upper levels - along with Talents - that correspond to Intrinsic Motivation: the extent to which our work is aligned with our Talents and Purpose. The Purpose level addresses the extent to which you feel connected to, or receive meaning from, your work.

To have a Purpose is to contribute to something greater than oneself. A Purpose is something that is never-ending, doesn't have a deadline, and which is not attainable in and of itself. As with Talents, Purpose is also a trait of well-being or eudaimonia and living life with one leads to greater happiness[14]. Consider a time when you volunteered for a cause or charity or offered to help a person or organization, which you felt was contributing to the greater good. The work may have been hard or even menial, but your contribution to the cause was repaid in the form of a feeling of greater Purpose for yourself.

People who are only goal-driven are often extremely action-oriented and become restless if they do not have many things going on at the same time. They may have everything they could wish for, but they still can't quite identify why they suffer from this restlessness. They just feel that something should be different. When you experience this kind of inner uneasiness, it is often because you are not connecting your unique contributions to something that is meaningful to you.

Almost everyone has at one point or another thought, "There must be more to life than this". We may feel a nagging dissatisfaction, but are unable to locate the source of this feeling. We may be uncertain of the choices we make, and whether they are contributing meaningfully to what we might achieve in life. Finding one's Purpose in life is one of the most transformational experiences we can have. Finding our Purpose enables us to experience true inner motivation, leaving us with a feeling of effortlessness and satisfaction.

This level is where you get ultimate insight into what it will take to achieve and sustain a state of flow – the condition of being in "the zone", completely absorbed, committed and even compelled to carry on[19,20]. We'll see that when our goals and choices are driven by, and clearly connected to, a sense of greater Purpose, we are able to contribute maximum performance and be rewarded with maximum satisfaction.

As a first step, we can take note of how our current goals and choices are guiding our life's path. Whether we are aware of it or not, our work is completely governed by the choices we make in relation to the goals we have. Even day-to-day routines are governed by goals. We go to work in order to make a living. We purchase resources in order to create a product. We hire staff, so that we are able to scale the business, etc.

Here, we investigate three different ways of working:

1. When your choices govern your goal
2. Letting your goal govern your choices
3. Letting your Purpose govern your goals and choices

Take an example from everyday life, which most of us recognize: Dinner.

## 1) When your choices govern your goal

In this instance, you have the undefined goal: "I want dinner". You drop by the supermarket on your way home, and have not really decided what you will cook for dinner. You go to the cooler and have a look. There is a wide range of poultry, fish and meat. What do you choose?

At that moment, your choices will be determined by a number of circumstantial factors, such as:

- Are you hungry?
- How much money are you carrying?
- What is your time frame for cooking?
- How many mouths do you have to feed?
- Are you in a good or bad mood?
- Are there special offers vying for your attention?
- How healthy do you want dinner to be?

All these in-the-moment factors will determine what you choose to put in your shopping basket. Let's say you are hungry and tired at the moment you search the cooler.

You are in a hurry and want to get it over with it as quickly as possible. You notice that ground beef is on offer, but it has a very high fat content. OK, so the fat content is high, but you are already visualizing pasta Bolognese on the table: easy, fast and cheap.

Your goal is now to have pasta Bolognese.

## 2) When your goal governs your choices

When your goal governs your choices, you are clear on what you want before you get started. Your choices will be a reflection of your goal. In this instance, you have defined the goal specifically: "I want fish with fresh asparagus and potatoes for dinner".

Now you are in a completely different situation: You can select your purchases quickly without being concerned with other products in the supermarket. This is the difference between:

- I want dinner (undefined, flexible)
- I want fish with asparagus and potatoes for dinner (defined, inflexible)

You are not distracted by in-the-moment factors because you are buying regardless of whether:

- It is on sale or not
- It takes a long time to cook or not
- You are in a good or bad mood

So it wouldn't be wrong to say that the shopping process is far less demanding. Yes, you may miss out on the special offer of the day, but shopping has been far easier. Being goal-oriented offers many benefits: You proceed with certainty, your efforts are efficient, and you are not distracted by doubt or alternative choices. You have consciously decided your direction even before you enter the supermarket. There are, however, at least two disadvantages to this approach: First, the danger of being so focused on a goal that you miss a better opportunity and second, you become paralyzed if something or someone is in your way of reaching your goal.

### 3) When your Purpose governs your goals and choices

Let's say you want to lose 10 pounds. You are highly motivated, and you eat healthily and exercise. Once you have dropped the 10 pounds and you have reached your goal, then what? Well, many people who have achieved this goal start gaining weight again. This happens, because they have reached their goal but haven't been clear about what they want to happen next. Alternatively, if your Purpose is a healthy lifestyle, you will be able to maintain motivation and weight-loss indefinitely.

A healthy way of life doesn't have a deadline. Rather it is an identifier: "I am a healthy person" or a state of being "I live healthily" - and your choices follow suit in the long term.

Of course you can still set yourself goals, but you will always have a higher Purpose to link your goals to. This is the difference between:

- I want dinner (undefined, flexible)
- I want fish with asparagus and potatoes for dinner (defined, inflexible)
- I live healthy (defined, flexibility)

By having the Purpose of "living healthily" you will be able to sort through the options you find yourself faced with in life. The process of shopping becomes much easier, as you have already rejected all the unhealthy options, yet at the same time, you are not locked into one particular option. You may never put a pound of ground beef with high fat content in your shopping basket, yet you can still choose between fish and chicken. One might say that you are combining the best of both worlds.

You may recognize this pattern in your own work and life. This approach certainly applied to me, as I lived the first 40 years of my life like this. Recall the story of my director pounding his fist on his desk, asking me what it would take to motivate me. I didn't know. Indeed, I was allowing my choices to govern my goals. When a new and interesting possibility showed up, I went with it. And when a different possibility occurred, well, then I went in that direction instead. But no matter which way I went, the pattern remained the same: I got bored after a short while and my motivation disappeared. My life was like a roller coaster, one moment up, the next down.

I was deeply frustrated by the fact that I was not happy all the time. I did have a goal for myself: I wanted to work in sales because I was clearly competent in that area. But I had not really determined whether I wanted to work with partner sales, direct sales, or as a sales manager. For this reason I jumped at whichever opportunity seemed interesting.

My goal was: 'I want to work with sales' (undefined, flexible)

My choices were made on the basis of momentary factors, which were in complete control of my life. And because there were so many possibilities, I was in constant doubt whether the choice I was about to make was a right one. But at the same time I almost made a virtue of not having a definite goal – "keeping my options open" as it were.

Similar patterns exist in organizations. Companies make a choice that provides, or stems from, short-term motivation because choices are controlled by momentary circumstances. And of course, we've all experienced the frustration of ditching one selection for the "next big thing" just as we're starting to get the hang of the last implementation. You might avoid feeling restricted and/or missing out on opportunities but, in the long run, letting your choices govern your goals can be complex, exhausting and, ultimately, unsatisfactory. The same goes for your career.

If your goal is: "I want to be a sales manager in IBM's enterprise software solutions", you will find it easy to dismiss job offers that will not lead you in the direction of that goal. This defined and inflexible goal is different from the undefined and flexible goal of "I want to work in sales."

When I look back on my many years in IT, I realize that I was most successful working for companies selling software solutions that helped clients optimize their sales processes. But because my goal was "I want to work in sales", I also accepted positions with companies that sold software that optimized technical processes. I quickly lost my motivation in those environments because I did not realize what was truly important to me.

If I had realized my Purpose at that time: "I help my customers optimize their sales processes" I would have avoided some of the job changes I made. And I would have kept up my motivation to a much larger extent. Here is the evolution of finding my purpose:

- I want to work in sales (undefined, flexible) and

- I want to be sales manager in IBM's enterprise software solutions. (defined, inflexible because there is only one of these positions) and

- I help my customers optimize their sales processes. (defined, flexible)

## Passion's role in Purpose

Essential to one's Purpose is the incorporation of one's passions. Passions, here, are defined as those activities or contributions that give you satisfaction, gratification, or a sense of accomplishment by engaging in them. For example, with my Purpose being to "help my customers to optimize their sales processes", it stands to reason that my passions might include:

- Optimizing sales processes

- Uncovering client Needs

- Maximizing return on investment

Passions are aspects of work and life that give positive meaning. Being aware of and incorporating them into one's Purpose results in a powerful cocktail for intrinsic motivation toward and guidance regarding life's choices.

# The wheel of Motivation

PURPOSE    NEEDS

WHEEL OF MOTIVATION

PASSIONS    TALENTS

WHEEL OF MOTIVATION©

It is important to remember that all our motivation factors are linked to each other. Imagine that the illustration at the left side is a wheel and each element in the wheel contains motivation. The higher the level of transferred motivation between the elements, the faster the wheel spins. But if one or more element is damaged, the wheel's ability to spin will be reduced or, worst case, it will stop spinning.

If we lack motivation, we should revisit our wheel of motivation to see what has changed and where we need to adjust in order to make the wheel spin fast again.

I discovered this myself not too long before I began writing this book. My work was nicely tied to my Purpose, which is "through neuropsychology I develop and catalyze new programs and methodologies that help people find their motivation." But as the business grew, I sometimes found myself lacking in motivation without really knowing why. The answer became obvious as I considered my change in focus from developing and catalyzing to managing an established business. Those two efforts require different competencies. I was now in a position where everyone looked to me for answers to everything.

I became the leader within every aspect of the business: "What is the strategy, what is the empirical data behind Motivation Factor, what are the key messages, how do we sell it, what are your plans, what will the infrastructure look like", etc. This new role was not giving me energy. In fact, it was becoming a full-fledged Energy Drainer.

When I revisited my Purpose, it became very clear to me that I was not utilizing two of my Talents "develop" and "catalyze". I was too busy maintaining and growing the business, but my motivation came from developing and catalyzing new programs and methodologies, and not from the other aspect of the business. In my case, raising awareness to the fact that it had been a long time since I had developed anything new made me take immediate action. I needed to allocate time to develop something new to get my motivation back.

# Working with Purpose

This section will outline the Motivation Factor approach to working with Purpose. There are four steps in this method, and exercises are included for each step.   The method is intended to be a conversation between two or more people, but it can work equally well if done individually. You are encouraged to try it out on yourself and colleagues.


## The key steps in working with Purpose

1.   Define the objective

2.   Uncover your passions

3.   Define your Purpose statement

4.   Taking ownership of the Purpose


## 1.   Define the objective

First of all, you need to decide in what context you want to do your Purpose statement. Is it to define yourself as a manager, in relation to a goal, or do you want to link it to company values?


## 2.   Uncover your passions

Once an objective has been defined, ask questions similar to the following to uncover your passions:

What do I really love about being a manager (or about this goal)?

In which situations am I at my best?

What comes naturally to me?

You will end up with a list of passions. You should choose the 2 or 3 that give you most energy to be part of your Purpose.

## 3. Define your Purpose statement

There are some guidelines that you need to keep in mind when you define your Purpose. The Purpose must:

- NOT be measurable and/or evidently attainable
- Be written in the present tense
- Contain the words "help" or "contribute" or similar
- Be linked to the stated Objective (e.g. you as a manager)
- Passions and/or Talents should be included in the Purpose Statement

## Example Cases

The following are four examples taken from Motivation Factor workshops where participants are led through the steps in working with their Purpose.

## EXAMPLE 1:

The objective was to define her Purpose in her role as a member of the management team.

| Passions | |
|---|---|
| 1 | Insight (communication, knowledge) |
| 2 | Peace (framework, process) |
| 3 | Openness (curiosity, listen, sense) |

| Purpose Statement |
|---|
| I contribute to the management team by bringing insight, peace and kindness and by encouraging openness. |

## EXAMPLE 2:

The objective was to define his Purpose in his role as a sales manager.

| Passions | |
|---|---|
| 1 | Motivation |
| 2 | Foster development |
| 3 | Customer focus |

| Purpose Statement |
|---|
| I contribute to foster a motivated sales team that makes customer focused decisions. |

## EXAMPLE 3:

The objective was to define his Purpose in his role as a manager.

| Passions | |
|---|---|
| 1 | Different competencies |
| 2 | Finding new ways |
| 3 | Performance |

| Purpose Statement |
|---|

Based on the different competencies in the team, I contribute to finding new ways of increasing our performance.

**EXAMPLE 4:**

The objective was to define her Purpose in her role as a coach.

| Passions | |
|---|---|
| 1 | Making choices |
| 2 | Creating clarity |
| 3 | Purpose |

| Purpose Statement |
|---|

I help people clarify their Purpose in order to make the right choice.

## 4. Taking ownership of the Purpose

Once the Purpose is defined, it is important that you take ownership of it. Here are some sample questions that you can ask yourself, once the Purpose statement is defined:

- When you look at this Purpose, how does it match the fulfillment of your Needs?

- Are any of your Needs threatened by the Purpose? Which ones and how?

- How are your Talents applied as part of this Purpose?

- How meaningful is this statement to you? Does it need more? Less?

- How do your Passions come into play? Can they be reflected more strongly?

- Read your Purpose aloud to me and imagine you are in a conversation, where you are selling yourself. How does it sound to you?

- How does it feel to say your Purpose out loud?

- What do you think, when you see your Purpose written in this way?

- Do you feel ownership of your Purpose – what can be changed and how?

- What helps you keep a strong focus on your Purpose?

- Where will you need to pay extra attention in order to succeed? How will you do this?

- What is different now that you have this Purpose?

- On a scale of one to ten, how motivated are you to succeed? What do you need to do to reach ten?

## Chapter summary

In this chapter, the concept of Purpose was introduced. For many, this is the most difficult level in the Hierarchy of Motivation to complete. That being said, it is the most rewarding level to get to and work with, as it is the culmination of all the work you have done in the Energy Drainer, Needs, and Talents workshops. The workshop steps will lead you through a series of exercises with the goal of defining your Purpose. To have a Purpose is to contribute to something greater than oneself and, in doing so, increasing our intrinsic motivation to even higher levels.

# Chapter 10:
## Motivation Lives in the Brain

As with all of our behaviors, whether simple or complex, motivation lives in the brain. Not only does it live in the brain, it is influenced by all of the other cognitive processes. In recent years, groundbreaking knowledge has been acquired regarding the connection between human behavior and brain processes.

Science has integrated research on the human mind and behavior (psychology) with research on the brain's anatomy and functions (neuroscience) in new ways. Additionally, advanced technologies such as functional magnetic resonance imaging (fMRI) have helped us to better understand the relationship between brain processes and our thoughts, emotions, sensations and behavior.

## Understanding the brain

To start, it would be helpful to understand a little more about the layout of the brain. The brain is an incredibly complex organ, but for the Purposes of understanding the neural underpinnings of The Motivation

Factor framework, the focus will be on cortical and subcortical areas involved in cognitive functions, emotions, and memory formation.

The subcortical areas of interest are the hypothalamus, amygdala and the hippocampus. Together these areas along with other evolutionarily older areas are collectively called the limbic system. The hypothalamus is located in the center of the brain and is involved in the control of involuntary body functions such as breathing, heart rate, and blood pressure[15]. The amygdala are almond-shaped groups of nuclei located deep in the brain near the center and play a pivotal role in the processing and formation of memories of stressful and emotionally charged experiences as opposed to normal episodic memories of daily events. Most of the emotional processing in the amygdala is in relation to negative or aversive events that result in fear[21]. The hippocampus is a bilateral brain region that resembles a seahorse in shape. It plays important roles in the formation of short and long-term memories, emotional responses, and spatial navigation, as well as regulating stress response[11].

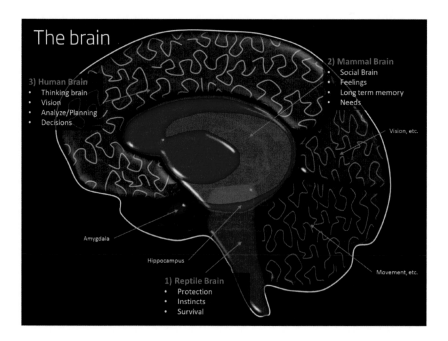

The brain

3) Human Brain
- Thinking brain
- Vision
- Analyze/Planning
- Decisions

2) Mammal Brain
  Social Brain
- Feelings
- Long term memory
- Needs

Vision, etc.

Amygdala

Hippocampus

1) Reptile Brain
- Protection
- Instincts
- Survival

Movement, etc.

The cerebral cortex of the brain is the outermost structure and evolutionarily the newest part of the brain. The prefrontal cortex (PFC), located in the front third of the brain, is involved in planning goal directed behavior, making decisions, governing social behavior, and in learning and memory[22]. It is referred to as the brain's executive controller or CEO, because this is where we create visions for the future, strategize, develop plans and tactics and determine which actions to put in place to reach our goals.

One of the hallmarks of the PFC is that it is flexible or plastic in what information it holds. In other words the circuitry (i.e. connections) of the PFC can be remodeled by experiences, both positive and negative, in ways that alter brain function[22]. It is this capacity that allows us to learn and to adapt to the changing world.

Each of these areas has specific functions, and it is the interplay or communication between the areas that determines our emotions, cognitive flexibility, and ultimately our motivation.

# Neuroscience behind the Energy Drainers and Needs

*If you are distressed by anything external, the pain is not due to the thing itself, but to your estimate of it; and this you have the power to revoke at any moment.*

Marcus Aurelius (Meditations)
Roman Emperor and Philosopher (121 AD - 180 AD)

The Energy and Needs levels of the Hierarchy of Motivation (Motivation Capability) are key in providing a personal understanding of why certain situations or behaviors have negative effects on our behavior and life.

As with Maslow's hierarchy of Needs, the individual must take responsibility for his or her Energy Drainers and the fulfilling of Needs in order to find happiness and motivation[2]. A large portion of the negative impact on day-to-day living manifests itself as stress. Knowing more about how the body reacts to stress and how to reduce its effects is fundamental to increasing motivation.

## The fight or flight stress response

Stress can come in many forms of averseness, such as a hostile manager, unpaid bills, an oncoming out-of-control car, or a predator trying to eat you. The near instantaneous fight or flight response of increased heart rate, sweating, and tensing muscles triggered by a life-threatening situation evolved as a survival mechanism, such as an out of control car veering towards you.

While potentially lifesaving, repeated or continuous activation (i.e. chronic stress) is harmful to the body, especially the brain. Unfortunately in today's fast paced competitive world, it is quite common to have the fight or flight response triggered many times a day. The negative implications such as moodiness, burnout, and feelings of being overwhelmed are usually due to the physiological reaction to stress.

## Subcortical areas involved in the stress response

A typical stress response follows the following path through different brain areas. Once sensory information from the eyes and/or ears reaches the amygdala, it is interpreted as being threatening or not. A distress signal is sent from the amygdala to the hypothalamus if danger or a threat is perceived. This distress signal initiates the coordinated release of hormones by the hypothalamus and other brain structures under its control.

One such hormone is adrenaline, which is released from the adrenal glands that sit on top of the kidneys. Adrenaline courses through the body causing increased heart rate and tensing of muscles. A second set of hormones implicated in the stress response is the glucocorticoids, with cortisol being the predominant one in humans. Once released, cortisol has widespread effects on the body, most of which involve redistributing energy resources to the areas of the body that need it the most (i.e. heart and brain) and away from less important areas (i.e. digestive and reproductive organs).

Once the threatening situation is no longer an issue, it is the elevated cortisol levels that help to turn off the fight or flight response. The stress response is entirely safe and normal if it occurs infrequently. One of the hallmarks of the stress response is that it is very fast, even faster than the visual processing centers of the brain, which explains why people can jump out of the way of an oncoming bicycle before they even know what they are seeing.

Essentially the rest of the brain is hijacked for the duration of the response, which historically made sense as it usually served to deal with a life-threatening circumstance. Today, this hijacking can be seen in employees who 'freeze' or have tunnel vision and can't adapt to changing environments.

Serious health problems occur when the stress response is triggered often or chronically (i.e. all the time). Even though the stress response exists to get out of life-threatening situations, it is important to realize that same cascade of hormones is released when the body overreacts to non-life-threatening situations such as traffic jams, annoying coworkers, and money issues. Without proper control, it is understandable that many people end up living with chronic stress. Negative consequences can include compromised immune response, eating problems, insomnia, aging, and cognitive dysfunction.

One structure of the brain that is particularly sensitive to cortisol is the hippocampus. Exposure to high levels of cortisol over long time periods, such as in chronic stress, has been shown to impair the formation of new memories, the recall of memories, and learning, and inhibit the growth of new neurons[11].

In addition, since the amygdala and hippocampus work together to generate emotional response and memories, it would be detrimental if either one is not functioning correctly. Damage to the hippocampus due to chronic stress can lead to moodiness, irritability, feeling overwhelmed, depression, poor judgment, and anxiety. It is not hard to understand why stressed employees are not motivated.

## Cortical area involved in the stress response

As with subcortical structures, the PFC is also affected by chronic stress. The main effect is that the flexibility to make and maintain circuitry is diminished, thereby diminishing the effectiveness of the PFC in learning, adapting to new situations or information, and decision making[17].

The PFC receives input from subcortical emotion structures (i.e. hippocampus and amygdala), as well as from many other sensory structures. It exerts its influence through what is called 'top-down control' by sending information back to sensory regions to alter perception and focus attention.

While the influence of the PFC on the rest of the brain can be great, it does need to be taught or shown through learning. Early on in learning a new task, the PFC has been shown to be active while consolidating the rules and intricacies of the new task and less active later on, once a task is well learned[16].

The Motivation Factor framework is a series of processes that will enable the user to teach his or her PFC to have a greater influence on the rest of the brain.

# Energy Drainers in the brain

Energy Drainers, as described in the chapter Impact of Energy Drainers, are essentially distractions that take you away from the task at hand or current goal. This interference can stem from either an external source such as a noisy work environment or internally generated by our thoughts.

Research has shown that whether the distractions are externally or internally generated, they interfere negatively with our ongoing cognitive and neural processes[9,10]. This can lead to compounding effects of the stress response, especially if the Energy Drainers persist over a long period of time.

External interferences cause distractions because they must either be ignored (i.e. bright blinking lights or a loud noise) or dealt with instead (i.e. a passenger talking to you while you are driving). Both responses require the brain to shift away from the current goal.

When distractions are to be ignored, the executive controller area of the brain, the PFC, is involved in actively suppressing the visual and auditory sensory areas to lessen the brain's response to the distractions[10]. When distractions require action such as responding to a text message while driving or working in a noisy office, the brain tries to multitask and do two cognitive tasks at once.

Evidence has shown repeatedly that the brain is not really able to multitask[23] and that it can be dangerous to attempt to do so, especially when driving[24]. The danger arises because the brain will switch to a serial processing mode, in which it will focus all resources on one task (i.e. texting) at the expense of another task (i.e. driving).

It is important to realize that the same neural systems (memory, attention, and decision making) that are involved in carrying out the current goal are also engaged in dealing with distractions. There is only so much brain capacity to go around.

The best way to deal with external distractions is to minimize them before they take over. This could explain the popularity of noise cancelling headphones in open concept offices and the campaigns to make texting and driving illegal.

Internally generated distractions in the form of intrusive thoughts, emotions, and urges are equally able to interfere with current goals[25]. It is these types of distractions that are most relevant to the Motivation Factor. As with externally generated interference, the result is that attention, memory and thought are disrupted from the original goal and become focused on the internal thoughts[10].

The more time spent thinking about Energy Drainers, the less time is spent thinking about the current goal. Surprisingly, one study found that people tended to be less happy when their minds were wandering than when they were not, even when they were thinking of pleasant topics[26]. In other words, their 'cluttered' minds took away from their ability to be happy.

Research into brain areas involved in the generation and control of internal distraction is an emerging field, and the roles of brain areas are still being worked out. Early research indicates that a specific set of brain areas, collectively known as the default network, are activated during internal directed or self-generated thought[27].

Self-generated thoughts do not always have a negative impact on the current goal, since these thoughts can be creative and insightful. It is when self-generated thought becomes disruptive (i.e. Energy Drainers), essentially hijacking your attention, that they are detrimental.

This could explain why people who are daydreaming are not as responsive to being called, since their attentiveness to the external world is suppressed. The key to efficient cognitive function is to have the correct balance and control over the internally directed and goal directed thought.

In the Motivation Factor framework, Energy Drainers are identified, classified, and options are generated in order to define actions for the future. By following the steps outlined in the workshop, the number of unwanted internally generated distractions should be reduced, thereby clearing the mind to focus on the current goals.

## Needs in the brain

The major difficulty when discussing your Needs is in figuring out what they are. This is where the Motivation Factor Indicator is instrumental by naming the individualized top five Needs. By combining awareness of our Needs and how to manage our emotional response to what we dislike in others, we can learn and take responsibility for ensuring that our Needs are met.

The process of working Needs, as well as Energy Drainers, begins with understanding how our emotions are regulated. When our Needs are not met, typically the stress response is triggered. Over time, this can have the detrimental effects listed above.

The Motivation Factor Needs workshop works to address how to reduce the triggering of the stress response when our Needs are not met by employing a form of emotional regulation.

Interestingly, the same brain areas that are involved in the stress response are involved in emotional generation and regulation.

## Emotional regulation

The ability to control emotions is vitally important to our mental and physical well-being. It is essential to manage emotional impulses for adaptive function in social contexts and to pursue life goals. The influence an individual has over his or her emotions and how s/he experiences and shows them is called emotion regulation.

Recent research by James J. Gross and colleagues[28-30] has led to a theoretical model of the process of emotion regulation, and it has been the topic of many theoretical and empirical experiments.

This model suggests that there are two main types of emotional regulation:

1. Cognitive change strategies and

2. Attentional control strategies

These two emotion regulation strategies have very different emotional and physiological consequences. Cognitive change strategies occur at the appraisal stage before our response has fully formed into a behavior and physiological response. Cognitive control involves altering the way you think about a situation in order to decrease its emotional impact. An example would be to view an insulting co-worker's comment as a sign that they are just tired as opposed to taking it personally.

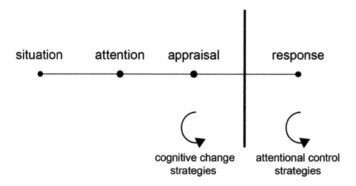

The four points of emotion generative process: 1) selection of situation, 2) deployment of attention, 3) appraisal, 4) modulation of experiential, behavioral, or physiological responses. The first three processes are before an emotional response and the fourth is the response. Modified from Gross and Thompson 2007.

In terms of Needs, this translates into understanding the Needs underlying our emotional response and changing the way we respond (i.e. not being angry with someone who has threatened one of our Needs).

Attentional control strategies occur at the time of response, once an emotion is already underway, and work by suppressing or inhibiting the outward signs of emotion, for instance smiling even though you are angry at a coworker who has threatened one of your Needs. The main difference between cognitive change strategies and attentional control strategies is that in the former the emotion you choose is changed, and in the latter the original emotion is felt but you work to control it.

Many studies have contrasted cognitive change strategies versus attentional control strategies[31,32]. Overall attentional control (suppression of response) has been shown to have negative consequences on both emotion regulation and physiology. In one experiment, individuals viewed a short film of a disgusting arm amputation[30].

The cognitive change strategy used in the study was reappraisal, where one group was told to view the film as if it were a medical teaching film, thereby framing the gory and disgusting segments as educational. The attentional control group was told to hide (suppress) their reaction to the film. A third group (control) just watched the film. When suppressing disgust-expressive emotions, individuals had increased heart rate and blood pressure (stress response). The reappraisal group did not show the same stress related physiological changes.

Attentional control strategy was also found to affect memory performance, whereas a cognitive change strategy did not[33]. The thinking is that the suppression of emotions requires constant self-monitoring and self-correction, which requires a continual use of cognitive capacity, leaving little room for other cognitive events to occur (i.e. the system gets overloaded trying to keep the emotions bottled up). Just think about the overloaded donkey in the Energy chapter.

The Needs Workshop of Motivation Factor invokes reappraisal to encourage participants to seek alternate interpretations and to make different judgments about emotional triggers. How it works is exemplified in the exercise where the participant's Top Five dislikes are paired with the Top Five Needs.  The dislikes all trigger the stress response and all the unwanted consequences because they are threatening personal Needs.

Once this realization occurs, the participant can begin to cognitively change through reappraisal their responses to triggers in the future. With reappraisal and understanding, threatening triggers are no longer threatening, and over time the elicited stress responses will diminish.

In Chapter 7, The Nature of Needs, a typical confrontation between my husband and daughter was described.  Put briefly, my husband would confront my daughter on the messiness of her room.  Given that their Needs are not the same, it would escalate into a major event.

Below is what would happen if my Husband implemented an attentional control strategy to suppress his response.

| Situation | Attention | Appraisal | Response |
|---|---|---|---|
| Husband fighting with daughter | Focuses his attention on the mess and repeated broken promises. | Anger is needed because the daughter has done this before. | Suppresses yelling at daughter, but still feels angry. |

In this case the attentional control strategy only alleviated the fighting and yelling.  The internal emotions were still there, and the father/daughter relationship did not improve.

Now here is what happened when my husband used a cognitive control strategy to reappraise the problems he was having with his daughter.

| Situation | Attention | Reappraisal strategy | Response |
|---|---|---|---|
| Husband fighting with daughter | Realizes that fighting is not optimal. Determines that his Needs for 'order' and 'honesty' are not being met, leading to his anger. | Considers daughter's Needs and realizes her Needs for 'freedom' and 'respect' are not being met, leading to her anger. Works on a solution that will not trigger the amygdala threat response. | Decides that having a conversation about the Needs conflict and taking responsibility for own Needs is a better approach. This involves explaining to his daughter why he would like her room to be cleaned. A compromise is reached without fighting or yelling. |

As you can see, the household was much calmer after the workshop, and my husband was able to control his emotions not through suppression but by understanding the Needs of everyone involved.

Cognitive change using reappraisal is a better way to regulate emotions as it impacts the emotion generative process before a response is made, thereby reducing the physiological impact of the chosen emotion[28,29,31]. In other words, with a little training, triggering the stress response and all its negative effects can be avoided.

## Reappraisal in the brain

Brain regions involved in emotional regulation have recently been studied using functional Magnetic Resonance Imaging[31,34]. These investigations have shown that areas of the PFC and anterior cingulate cortices (ACC) are active during the expression of emotions and importantly, some of the areas have connections to the subcortical limbic system (i.e. amygdala).

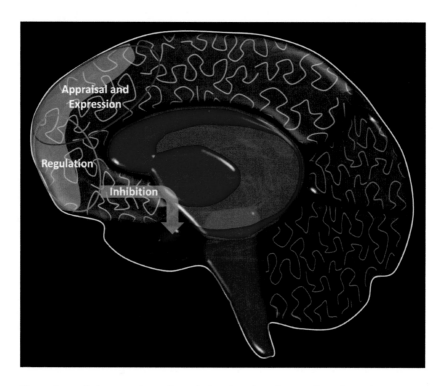

Illustration of the putative roles of the dorsal and ventral prefrontal and anterior cingulate cortices in the appraisal and expression of emotions. The dorsal regions (in red) are more involved in appraisal of emotions and the ventral regions (in blue) have regulatory roles through interconnections with the limbic system. Reappraisal involves the dorsal regions first, then the ventral regions. Modified from Etkin et al. 2011.

The dorsal PFC area and ACC (orange circle in figure) were active whenever participants were reappraising their emotional responses[31,35].

This suggests that the cognitive change strategy was occurring in these areas by altering the choice of emotional expression.

The ventral PFC areas (blue circle in figure) were active whenever the reappraisal by the participants resulted in the down-regulation of emotional response.    This was mirrored by a decrease in amygdala activation, suggesting that these executive control areas were inhibiting or stopping amygdala activation, thereby lessening negative emotion.

Anatomical studies have shown that there are indeed connections between the ventral PFC and the amygdala.  Going back to the model of emotional processing, this means that the cognitive change strategy (reappraisal) was able to dampen negative emotions before they were fully generated by the limbic system.

## Summary of Energy Drainers and Needs in the brain

The first two level of the Hierarchy of Motivation are about awareness. More specifically, awareness of what is preventing you from attaining your goal and what your Needs are.

Neurophysiologically, this awareness translates into more efficient use of the processing power of the brain by minimizing distractions and reducing the impact of triggered stress responses. Not only does this improve cognitive abilities and overall health, it opens the mind (so to speak) to progress onto the final two levels of the hierarchy, Talents and Purpose.

# Neuroscience behind Talents and Purpose

The two upper levels in the Hierarchy of Motivation, Talents and Purpose, correspond to Intrinsic Motivation. That is the extent to which you feel your work and life are aligned with your inherent qualities, your passions and with what you find meaningful. Tapping into your Talents and being clear about your Purpose is where growth, learning and real change occur. And as with the other levels of the Hierarchy of Motivation, they manifest in the brain.

To further explore the neuroscience of Talents and Purpose, an understanding of happiness and well-being is needed. It is within these complex notions of human behavior that Talents and Purpose reside. Since Aristotle and most recently in the field of positive psychology[13,20,36], well-being or happiness has been thought to consist of two distinct aspects: the experience of pleasure (hedonia) and the notion of a life well lived (eudaimonia)[37].

Hedonia, from the Greek word for pleasure, is the subjective short-term experience of happiness (i.e. eating ice cream or looking at pictures of your children). In contrast, eudaimonia, from the Greek word for happiness or welfare, is defined as a life well lived, embedded in meaningful values, together with a sense of commitment in that life[38]. Eudaimonia consists of the words 'eu', which translates to 'good', and 'daimōn', which translates to 'spirit'.

Talents and Purpose as described in the Hierarchy of Motivation are more in line with the life-well-lived or eudaimonic aspects of happiness and well-being. This has been shown and validated by one of the most widely used measures of eudaimonia: the *Ryff Scales of Psychological Well-being* developed by Carol Ryff[13]. This measure divides eudaimonia into six dimensions:

1. **Purpose in life:** The extent to which respondents felt their lives had meaning, Purpose, and direction

2. **Autonomy:** Whether they viewed themselves living by their personal convictions

3. **Personal growth:** The extent to which they were using their personal Talents and potential

4. **Environmental mastery:** How well they were managing their life situations

5. **Positive relationships:** Depth of connection they had with others, and

6. **Self-acceptance:** The knowledge and acceptance they had of themselves.

Finding Purpose and utilizing Talents (personal growth) are two of the dimensions upon which well-being is predicated.

Both hedonia and eudaimonia are important in overall happiness and well-being. Even though their definitions are quite different, they are correlated in happy people, with most people who rated their life satisfaction as 'pretty to very happy' also rating their current hedonic mood as positive[14].

Positive hedonic states have been shown to attenuate the perceived difficulty of demanding tasks, lessen the impact of adverse events, and foster behavioural flexibility[7]. This is why working with Energy and Needs (Motivation Capabilities) and building awareness of your cognitive abilities acts as the foundation or basis for building a positive hedonic state. Just think of all the situations when you felt that you had the capability and were on top of things, and how easily you accomplished your goals.

In addition, evidence suggests that people who have a Purpose (meaning and direction in life) have lower cardiovascular risk, reduced risk of mild cognitive impairments and slower rate of cognitive decline[8]. Taken together, being happy and having Purpose in life act as shields against negativity and poor health.

## Talents and Purpose in the brain

Although there is evidence that eudaimonic well-being and physical health are linked[6], there has been little research on the brain areas and neural mechanisms responsible for this link. To date, neuroscience studies have primarily focused on subjective pleasures such as 'liking', since it is easier to assess if a participant 'likes' or 'dislikes' a picture or a taste.

Another advantage is that hedonic reactions can occur on very short time scales (i.e. seconds to minutes) as opposed to the long time scales of eudaimonic well-being (i.e. months to years). Researchers are hopeful that knowing more about the brain mechanisms involved in hedonic well-being will lead to insights into eudaimonic well-being.

There is evidence to suggest that the brain mechanisms involved in subjective hedonic pleasures (e.g. food and sexual pleasures) do indeed overlap with more eudaimonia-like pleasures (e.g. monetary, artistic, Purpose)[38].

Surprisingly, there is also considerable overlap with the cortical and subcortical brain regions involved in emotional regulation and reappraisal, suggesting that our current state of happiness can influence our emotional responses and vice versa.

## Hedonic reward circuits

Many subcortical and cortical areas have been shown to respond to pleasurable experiences. The subcortical areas include the nucleus accumbens of the striatum, the ventral pallidum and areas of the brainstem. The cortical areas include the orbitofrontal, prefrontal, cingulate, and insular cortices.

All of these areas have also been shown to be important in the encoding of reward and reward seeking behavior. It is thought that the hedonic and/or eudaimonic circuits could reside within this larger reward circuit [39].

## Eudaimonic circuits

The current approach to investigating eudaimonia is to use the *Ryff Scales of Psychological Well-being*[13] to first assess the general well-being of participants. Brain activity is then inferred using fMRI and compared between groups with different levels of eudaimonia.

One such study found a particular area, the insular cortex, scaled in size with increasing eudaimonia[37]. This area has been implicated in self-awareness, regulation of body states, and decision-making in regards to body state[37]. Another study determined that participants with lower eudaimonia had increased amygdala activation (i.e. stress response) when shown negative images as compared to participants with higher eudaimonia[40].

This means that people with lower eudaimonia (i.e. less well-being) had stronger negative emotional responses to images than people who had higher eudaimonia (i.e. greater well-being). A more recent study shows that participants who reported higher eudaimonia had lower cortisol levels[18]. Recall that cortisol is released during a fight or flight stress response and that lower cortisol levels would suggest less stress.

Taken together, the ability to maintain a positive outlook (higher eudaimonia) even during adverse events reduces the impact of the stress response. While more research is required to fully understand eudaimonia, it seems as if the same executive control areas in the prefrontal cortex that are involved in suppressing or dampening negative emotions are involved in enabling eudaimonia.

## Summary of the Talents and Purpose in the brain

The upper two levels of the Hierarchy of Motivation are about growth. When you do what you love to do and feel that you contribute to something larger than yourself, you are much more productive, flexible and creative.  In fact, you are less likely to get caught up in negative thoughts that can impede progress and pull you down. By following the Motivation Factor workshops on Talents and Purpose, you will learn the tools to smile even when things can be challenging, yet without suppressing your emotions.

The eudaimonic traits of purpose in life and personal growth in the *Ryff Scales of Psychological Well-being*[13] fit with the concept of intrinsic motivation as outlined in the Hierarchy of Motivation. Similarly, the eudaimonic traits of environmental mastery and autonomy relate to the notion of Motivation Capabilities. The outcome of working with the Motivation Factor Framework is enhanced self-acceptance and positive relationships, both components of eudaimonic well-being.

# Chapter summary

Motivation crumbles starting with the Energy Drainers that distract from the current goal, clutter the mind, and waste resources. Next, Needs not being met further hinders motivation by invoking the stress response that hijacks the brain. When this occurs, it is almost impossible to live with a greater Purpose in mind and to use our Talents effectively. Together this makes us less resistant to setbacks while further reducing our motivation. Not to mention the short and long-term effects on physical health and well-being.

In this chapter, the relevant brain areas and circuits thought to be involved in the Hierarchy of Motivation were reviewed. While not an exhaustive study, our goal was for you to come away with a sense that the four levels of the Hierarchy of Motivation are connected and build on each other, not only in the Motivation Factor Framework but also in the brain.

As with many frameworks that require learning and change, the proof is in the trying. We are confident that by tapping into established neural circuits and behaviors; the positive changes of increased personal awareness and personal growth can be attained by anyone who tries. It is our hope that we have convinced you that not only can the brain be trained; it can be motivated!

# References

1. Maslow, A. H. A theory of human motivation. *Psychol. Rev.* **50,** 370 (1943).

2. Maslow, A. H. *Toward a psychology of being.* (D Van Nostrand, 1962).

3. Herzberg, F., Mausner, B. & Snyderman, B. B. *The motivation to work.* (Wiley, 1959).

4. Pink, D. *Drive: The Surprising Truth About What Motivates Us.* (Penguin Group (USA), 2011).

5. Iidaka, T., Harada, T. & Sadato, N. Forming a negative impression of another person correlates with activation in medial prefrontal cortex and amygdala. *Soc. Cogn. Affect. Neurosci.* **6,** 516–525 (2011).

6. Ryff, C. D. Psychological Well-Being Revisited: Advances in the Science and Practice of Eudaimonia. *Psychother. Psychosom.* **83,** 10–28 (2014).

7. Steenbergen, H. van, Band, G. P. H., Hommel, B., Rombouts, S. A. R. B. & Nieuwenhuis, S. Hedonic Hotspots Regulate Cingulate-driven Adaptation to Cognitive Demands. *Cereb. Cortex* (2014).

8. Schaefer, S. M. *et al.* Purpose in Life Predicts Better Emotional Recovery from Negative Stimuli. *PLoS ONE* **8,** (2013).

9. Clapp, W. C. & Gazzaley, A. Distinct mechanisms for the impact of distraction and interruption on working memory in aging. *Neurobiol. Aging* **33,** 134–148 (2012).

10. Mishra, J., Anguera, J. A., Ziegler, D. A. & Gazzaley, A. in *Prog. Brain Res.* (Merzenich, M. M., Nahum, M. & Van Vleet, T. M.) **Volume 207,** 351–377 (Elsevier, 2013).

11. Kim, J. J. & Diamond, D. M. The stressed hippocampus, synaptic plasticity and lost memories. *Nat. Rev. Neurosci.* **3,** 453–462 (2002).

12. Kalbfleisch, M. L. Functional neural anatomy of talent. *Anat. Rec. B. New Anat.* **277B,** 21–36 (2004).

13. Ryff, C. D. Happiness is everything, or is it? Explorations on the meaning of psychological well-being. *J. Pers. Soc. Psychol.* **57,** 1069–1081 (1989).

14. Kesebir, P. & Diener, E. In Pursuit of Happiness: Empirical Answers to Philosophical Questions. *Perspect. Psychol. Sci.* **3,** 117–125 (2008).

15. Kandel, E., Schwartz, J. & Jessel, T. *Principles of Neural Science.* (McGraw-Hill Professional, 2000).

16. Seger, C. A. & Miller, E. K. Category Learning in the Brain. *Annu. Rev. Neurosci.* **33,** 203–219 (2010).

17. McEwen, B. S. & Morrison, J. H. The Brain on Stress: Vulnerability and Plasticity of the Prefrontal Cortex over the Life Course. *Neuron* **79,** 16–29 (2013).

18. Heller, A. S. *et al.* Sustained Striatal Activity Predicts Eudaimonic Well-Being and Cortisol Output. *Psychol. Sci.* **24,** 2191–2200 (2013).

19. Csikszentmihalyi, M. *Flow: The Psychology of Optimal Experience.* (Harper Perennial Modern Classics, 2008).

20. Seligman, M. E. P. & Csikszentmihalyi, M. Positive psychology: An introduction. *Am. Psychol.* **55,** 5–14 (2000).

21. Fernando, A. B. P., Murray, J. E. & Milton, A. L. The amygdala: securing pleasure and avoiding pain. *Front. Behav. Neurosci.* **7,** (2013).

22. Miller, E. K. The prefontral cortex and cognitive control. *Nat. Rev. Neurosci.* **1,** 59–65 (2000).

23. Nijboer, M., Taatgen, N. A., Brands, A., Borst, J. P. & van Rijn, H. Decision Making in Concurrent Multitasking: Do People Adapt to Task Interference? *PLoS ONE* **8,** e79583 (2013).

24. Just, M. A., Keller, T. A. & Cynkar, J. A decrease in brain activation associated with driving when listening to someone speak. *Brain Res.* **1205,** 70–80 (2008).

25. Beauregard, M., Lévesque, J. & Bourgouin, P. Neural Correlates of Conscious Self-Regulation of Emotion. *J. Neurosci.* **21,** RC165–RC165 (2001).

26. Killingsworth, M. A. & Gilbert, D. T. A Wandering Mind Is an Unhappy Mind. *Science* **330,** 932–932 (2010).

27. Andrews-Hanna, J. R. The Brain's Default Network and Its Adaptive Role in Internal Mentation. *The Neuroscientist* **18,** 251–270 (2012).

28. Gross, J. J. Emotion regulation in adulthood: Timing is everything. *Curr. Dir. Psychol. Sci.* **10,** 214–219 (2001).

29. Gross, J. J. & Thompson, R. A. Emotion regulation: Conceptual foundations. *Handb. Emot. Regul.* **3,** 24 (2007).

30. Gross, J. J. Antecedent- and response-focused emotion regulation: Divergent consequences for experience, expression, and physiology. *J. Pers. Soc. Psychol.* **74,** 224–237 (1998).

31. Kohn, N. *et al.* Neural network of cognitive emotion regulation — An ALE meta-analysis and MACM analysis. *NeuroImage* **87,** 345–355 (2014).

32. Ochsner, K. N. & Gross, J. J. The cognitive control of emotion. *Trends Cogn. Sci.* **9,** 242–249 (2005).

33. Richards, J. M. & Gross, J. J. Emotion regulation and memory: The cognitive costs of keeping one's cool. *J. Pers. Soc. Psychol.* **79,** 410–424 (2000).

34. Etkin, A., Egner, T. & Kalisch, R. Emotional processing in anterior cingulate and medial prefrontal cortex. *Trends Cogn. Sci.* **15,** 85–93 (2011).

35. Kalisch, R. The functional neuroanatomy of reappraisal: Time matters. *Neurosci. Biobehav. Rev.* **33,** 1215–1226 (2009).

36. Huta, V. in *Best Us Posit. Psychol. Perspect. Eudaimonic Funct.* (Waterman, A.) pp. 139–158 (APA Books, 2013).

37. Lewis, G. J., Kanai, R., Rees, G. & Bates, T. C. Neural correlates of the 'good life': eudaimonic well-being is associated with insular cortex volume. *Soc. Cogn. Affect. Neurosci.* (2013).

38. Kringelbach, M. L. & Berridge, K. C. Towards a functional neuroanatomy of pleasure and happiness. *Trends Cogn. Sci.* **13,** 479–487 (2009).

39. Berridge, K. C. & Kringelbach, M. L. Neuroscience of affect: brain mechanisms of pleasure and displeasure. *Curr. Opin. Neurobiol.* **23,** 294–303 (2013).

40. Van Reekum, C. M. *et al.* Individual Differences in Amygdala and Ventromedial Prefrontal Cortex Activity are Associated with Evaluation Speed and Psychological Well-being. *J. Cogn. Neurosci.* **19,** 237–248 (2007).

# About the Author

**Helle Bundgaard** is the founder of Motivation Factor Institute.

Helle has 20+ years' of leadership experience as an international sales and business development executive in the software industry. In 2003 she decided to leave her job to pursue her passions and delving deeply into studies of motivation, psychology and neuroscience.

Her work has been focused around bridging the gap from lab brain research to developing practical and applicable management tools for use in a business context. This has led to the development of online assessments that reveals individual fundamental motivation factors, and company surveys that measures intrinsic motivation and Motivation Capabilities.

Helle has successfully conducted hundreds of workshops and executive coaching sessions all over the world. She has built a thriving business in Europe and the U.S. applying the Motivation Factor framework in different line of business and organizations. Her humor and ability to involve an audience makes her a requested keynote speaker,

Additionally Helle is associated with the Institute of Management Development (IMD) in Switzerland working with faculty in delivering leadership programs.

# About the Co-Author

**Jefferson Roy** is a neuroscientist with 20 years of research experience. Jefferson received his PhD from McGill University in Montreal, Canada. He traveled to the Massachusetts Institute of Technology in Cambridge, USA to further his training as a Post-doctoral Associate. Currently, Jefferson is a Research Scientist in the laboratory of Professor Earl Miller at The Picower Institute for Learning and Memory at MIT. His work focuses on the neuronal mechanisms of cognitive flexibility during goal-directed behavior, in other words how does the brain decide what we do. Jefferson has published over ten scientific manuscripts in peer-reviewed journals and his given many presentations at international scientific meetings.

Jefferson is also the founder of Muddled Mind Consulting. As the principal consultant, he has been providing quality neuroscience based technical help to many firms and organization. Prior work has work included writing whitepapers, data analysis, grant writing, as well as educational content creation.

Jefferson has been a member of The Expert Panel for Motivation Factor Institute since 2013.

Manufactured by Amazon.ca
Bolton, ON

11008805R00083